LUTHER AND STAUPITZ

LUTHER AND STAUPITZ

An Essay in the Intellectual Origins of the Protestant Reformation

by DAVID C. STEINMETZ

Duke Monographs in Medieval and Renaissance Studies number 4

DUKE UNIVERSITY PRESS   Durham, North Carolina   1980

Library of Congress Cataloging in Publication Data

Steinmetz, David Curtis.
  Luther and Staupitz.

  (Duke monographs in medieval and Renaissance
studies; no. 4)
  Includes bibliographical references and index.
    1. Luther, Martin, 1483–1546. 2. Staupitz,
Johann von, d. 1524. I. Title. II. Series.
BR329.S73   230'.41   80–23007
ISBN 0–8223–0447–3

To FRANZ HILDEBRANDT

Atque hoc posteris testatum esse volui, ut siqua ex meis scriptis ad eos perveniet utilitas, aliqua ex parte abs te manasse agnoscant.

CONTENTS

ABBREVIATIONS

AKG   Arbeiten zur Kirchengeschichte
ARG   *Archiv für Reformationsgeschichte*
BB   Beiträge zur Geschichte der Philosophie und Theologie des Mittelalters (Münster i.W., 1891–)
BoA   [Bonner Ausgabe] *Luthers Werke in Auswahl,* ed. Otto Clemen, 8 vols. (Bonn and Berlin, 1912ff.)
Hiob *Staupitz, Tübinger Predigten, Quellen und Forschungen zur Reformationsgeschichte,* Vol. 8, ed. Georg Buchwald and Ernst Wolf (Leipzig, 1927)
HTR   *Harvard Theological Review*
JTS   *Journal of Theological Studies*
Kn.   J.F.K. Knaake, *Johannis Staupitii, opera quae reperiri poterunt omnia: Deutsche Schriften,* Vol. 1 (Potsdam, 1867)
Libellus *Libellus de executione eterne predestinacionis* (Nuremberg, 1517)
PL   *Patrologia Latina,* ed. J. P. Migne (Paris, 1844–1890)
QFRG Quellen und Forschungen zur Reformationsgeschichte
Steinbach *Wendelini Steinbach, Opera Exegetica quae supersunt omnia: Volumen I, Commentarius in Epistolam S. Pauli ad Galatas,* ed. Helmut Feld (Mainz, 1976)
SMRT Studies in Medieval and Reformation Thought
WA   *D. Martin Luthers Werke: Kritische Gesamtausgabe* (Weimar, 1883–)
WAB   *D. Martin Luthers Werke: Briefwechsel* (Weimar, 1930–70)
WATR *D. Martin Luthers Werke: Tischreden* (Weimar, 1912–21)
ZKG   *Zeitschrift für Kirchengeschichte*

PREFACE

This book had its origin in a conversation with Professor Leif Grane at the Fourth International Congress for Luther Research in St. Louis in August 1971. Professor Grane suggested in his own characteristically quiet and diffident way that I ought to finish what I had begun in my earlier study of the theology of John Staupitz by examining the relationship between Staupitz and Luther. Anyone who has ever read the large and complicated body of literature on the young Luther will understand the reasons for my hesitation to do so. But Professor Grane's encouragement came at just that moment when I had finished one project and was about to start another. Sometimes a nudge is all that is needed to set us off in a direction which we had already half decided we wanted to explore.

Portions of this study have been read as papers to audiences at the universities of Geneva, Tübingen, Cambridge, Duke, Bonn, Virginia, North Carolina, Wisconsin, and Harvard and at meetings of the American Historical Association, the American Society of Church History, and the American Society for Reformation Research. It was completed with the aid of grants from the Duke University Research Council, the American Council of Learned Societies, the John Simon Guggenheim Memorial Foundation, the Andrew W. Mellon Foundation, and the Arthur Vining Davis Foundation. Special thanks are also due to Dean Thomas A. Langford of the Duke University Divinity School, who arranged my schedule in such a way as to allow greater freedom for writing and research.

Principal Michael Skinner and the staff of Wesley House, Cambridge, provided me with a quiet haven for study in the academic year 1977–78 and Professor Gordon Rupp of Emmanuel College opened the resources of Cambridge University to me. Cambridge has always been hospitable to Reformation studies and one has only to mention the names of such scholars as Gordon Rupp, Norman Sykes, Franz Hildebrandt, and Philip Watson to make clear how indebted English-speaking students of Luther are to Cambridge men.

This book has profited from conversations with a great many historians, not all of whom were aware at the time that their observations were grist for my mill. I would be very negligent indeed were I not to recall with pleasure conversations with H. C. Erik Midelfort, Leif Grane, E. Gordon Rupp, Mark U. Edwards, Heiko A. Oberman, Richard Wetzel, Steven E.

Ozment, George H. Williams, Ian Siggins, Lothar Graf zu Dohna, Scott H. Hendrix, and Edward P. Mahoney as important for the final shape of the argument in this study. In addition Professors Rupp, Edwards, Siggins, and Mahoney did me the very great kindness of reading my manuscript and commenting on it. It is customary to absolve one's friends of any responsibility for the errors in interpretation one may have committed and I do freely absolve them, though not without gratitude for the positive and often hidden contributions they made.

Sections of the first, third, and fifth chapters of this book appeared in a somewhat different form in essays published in the *Concordia Theological Monthly*, the *Archiv für Reformationsgeschichte*, and *The Sixteenth Century Journal* and are reprinted here by permission of the editors of those journals. Special thanks are owed to Mr. J. Samuel Hammond, Music Librarian at Duke University, who assumed the major role in the preparation of the index for this volume.

LUTHER AND STAUPITZ

I. INTRODUCTION

The relationship between Martin Luther and his superior in the Augustinian Order, John Staupitz, is a subject of enduring interest to Reformation historians. Among the influences on the young Luther, both real and imagined, Staupitz is clearly one of the most important. By Luther's own testimony the influence of Staupitz on his early theological and religious development was profound,[1] even if that testimony must be balanced against other more grudging words of criticism.[2] It was Staupitz, after all, who forced the unwilling Luther to earn his theological doctorate,[3] who counseled him in his "trials" (*Anfechtungen*),[4] who protected him in the early stages of his attack on indulgences[5]—indeed, who led him to a fresh interpretation of the meaning of penance[6] and who therefore set him on the road to Reformation.

Luther, who was always grateful by nature[7] and as generous in his praise of friends as he was harsh in his condemnation of enemies, remarked to his students that he had received nothing from Erasmus (which is not true), but everything from Staupitz (which is, to say the least, doubtful).[8] The last letter Luther wrote to Staupitz, though it is severely

---

1. "Staupicius hat die doctrinam angefangen," Luther, *WATR* 2, Nr. 526 (Spring 1533).

2. "Literas Staupitii non intelligo, nisi quod spiritu inanissimas video, ac non, ut solebat, scribit; Dominus revocet eum," Luther to W. Link (Wittenberg, 19 Dec. 1522) Enders 4, 39. Cf. Luther to W. Link (Wittenberg, 7 Feb. 1525), Enders 5, 122; "Remitto Staupitium: frigidulus est, sicut semper fuit, et parum vehemens. Fac, quod libet, indignus non est luce et publico libellus, cum tot monstra quotidie prodeant et vendantur."

3. Luther tells the story of his resistance to earning a theological doctorate many times during his life. Cf. *WATR* 1, Nr. 885; 2, Nr. 2255; 4, Nr. 3924, Nr. 4091; 5, Nr. 5371.

4. "Inn disen gedancken oder anfechtungen stecken, So were mihrs Ja von hertzen leidt, denn ich etwa auch drinnen gestecket. Undt wo mihr D. Staupitz, oder viel mehr Gott durch Doctor Staupitz, nicht heraus geholffen hette, so were ich darinn ersoffen undt langst in der helle," Luther to Count Albrecht of Mansfeld (Wittenberg, 23 Feb. 1542), Enders 14, 188f.

5. Cf. Heinrich Boehmer, *Martin Luther: Road to Reformation* (New York: Meridian Books, 1957), pp. 230–44.

6. Luther, "Begleitschreiben zu den resolutiones an Staupitz" (Wittenberg, 30 May 1518), *WA* 1, 525ff.

7. See in this connection the old but still important essay by Karl Holl, "Luthers Urteile über sich selbst," *Gesammelte Aufsätze zur Kirchengeschichte I: Luther* (Tübingen, 1921), pp. 381–419.

8. "Ex Erasmo nihil habeo. Ich hab al mein ding von Doctor Staupitz; der hatt mir occasionem geben," *WATR* 1, Nr. 173 (Feb. or Mar. 1532).

critical of the stance Staupitz has taken with respect to the Reformation,[9] nevertheless sounds the same note of indebtedness and deep gratitude. Not Luther, says the letter, but Staupitz first kindled the light which is now shining in the darkness.[10] If Luther is to be believed, then Staupitz is not merely a forerunner but the father of the Protestant Reformation.

Historians have reason to be skeptical of praise as generous as this, however much they may sympathize with the motivation which lies behind it. Luther's statements are certainly exaggerated. His memories of Staupitz are dilated by time and affection. Yet the plain fact remains that Luther perceived Staupitz as a crucial influence in his development as a theologian and reformer. What that perception implies and to what extent that perception is justified are problems the historian cannot sidestep. The significance of John Staupitz for the development of Martin Luther is an inescapable and, as yet, unsolved problem for Reformation research.

1. *Initial Difficulties*

Unraveling the relationship between Staupitz and Luther has never been easy and one can understand the reluctance of historians to attempt it. Luther's own witness concerning the influence of Staupitz is of two kinds: contemporary evidence from the period prior to Staupitz's death in 1524, such as the letter to Staupitz which accompanies the *Resolutions* of 1518,[11] and much later reflections, dating principally from the 1530s and from the convivial and informal setting of the *Tabletalk*. These two sources of evidence do not contradict each other, but more is claimed in the *Tabletalk* than can easily be established in the earlier materials.

That is not to say that the contemporary evidence does not establish

---

9. "Ego plane non desinam optare et orare, quam ut alienus a Cardinale tuo et papatu fias, sicut ego sum, imo sicut et tu fuisti," *WAB* 3.156. Nr. 659.36–38 (17 Sept. 1523).

10. "Sed nos certe etiamsi desivimus tibi grati ac placiti esse, tamen tui non decet esse immemores et ingratos, per quem primum coepit euangelii lux de tenebris splendescere in cordibus nostris," *WAB* 3.155–56. Nr. 659.5–8 (17 Sept. 1523).

11. Ernst Wolf, comparing this *Begleitschreiben* with the important preface to Luther's Latin writings of 1545 in which Luther also speaks of his *Turmerlebnis*, observes: "Sie wird darin gesehen, daß der Brief an Staupitz eine 'Dublette' zu Bericht der praefatio von 1545 darstellen würde, wenn Luther durch Staupitz und dessen Bußanschauung zum amor iustitiae geführt worden sein sollte." Ernst Wolf, *Staupitz und Luther, Ein Beitrag zur Theologie des Johannes von Staupitz und deren Bedeutung für Luthers theologischen Werdegang*, QFRG 9 (Leipzig, 1927), p. 253.

some extremely important facts about the relationship between Staupitz and Luther. It would be difficult to find a more important document for clarifying the nature of their relationship than the *Resolutions* of 1518. But to an uncomfortable extent historians are forced to rely on the later and less reliable *Tabletalk* for insights into the relationship between the two men.

Furthermore, there are gaps in the evidence at several crucial points. It is possible to state with great certainty what was the content of Staupitz's theology in 1498 and to affirm that there is no radical discontinuity between his theology in 1498 and 1512, the next period from which we have literary evidence.[12] Nevertheless, there are changes in his theology over this decade, changes which may have occurred prior to 1512, the period in which, by Luther's own testimony, the advice of Staupitz and his counsel in Luther's "trials" are especially important. We are forced to compare the earliest writings from Staupitz's pen (1497–98) with the earliest writings from Luther (1509), well aware of the fact that a decade has intervened in which we have no substantial literary evidence from Staupitz.

Luther did not hear the sermons on Job which Staupitz preached in Tübingen, though he may have heard the wry joke about them which Staupitz is alleged to have told at his own expense. According to one source Staupitz is believed to have said that he stopped preaching on Job at about the tenth or eleventh chapter when he came to the realization that he was afflicting Job with a worse plague than boils.[13] The sermons are certainly dry reading when compared with Staupitz's direct and simple sermons at Nonnberg or his theologically rich homilies at Nuremberg. The story, though it may have no foundation in fact,[14] nevertheless has a certain ring of truth about it.

Luther did not hear these dry sermons nor is there any reason to believe that he ever saw a manuscript of them. Indeed, there is no surviving evidence that Luther ever heard Staupitz lecture or preside at a disputation in Wittenberg. Staupitz's earliest influence on Luther seems to have been exercised exclusively through pastoral conversation. The only record of those conversations was preserved in Luther's memory. Staupitz does not

12. I argue this case in my *Misericordia Dei, The Theology of Johannes von Staupitz in Its Late Medieval Setting*, SMRT 4 (Leiden: E. J. Brill, 1968), p. 34.

13. The anecdote is recounted by Joh. Manlius in his *Locorum communium collectanea* (Basel, 1563), 3:14, and is reprinted by Otto Scheel, *Martin Luther, Vom Katholizismus zur Reformation* (Tübingen, 1917), 2:400.

14. Scheel believes that the story is not very probable. *Luther*, 2:194.

refer to them and there is no contemporary account of them by a third party.[15] Thus for the period in which Luther was most clearly under the influence of Staupitz and when there can be no real question of Luther's influence on Staupitz, the relevant evidence is tantalizingly scarce.

The most complete contemporary evidence for the relationship between Staupitz and Luther dates from the period 1512–24, also a critical period in Luther's theological development, yet a period in which Luther and Staupitz are in infrequent contact with each other. Luther's theology is developing rapidly during these years in new and independent directions. While Staupitz may have planted seeds in Luther's mind which only began to bear fruit after 1512, Staupitz is no longer exercising an immediate personal influence on his successor to the chair of biblical studies at the University of Wittenberg. Luther does, of course, read treatises by Staupitz and attempts without very much success to maintain an active correspondence with his old confessor. Just as the period before 1512 was marked by the influence of Staupitz on Luther through conversation—sometimes painfully blunt conversation at that—the period from 1512 to 1524 is characterized by severely restricted personal contact. Luther, at least, has nothing to say about significant pastoral or theological conversations from this period apart from one exchange which may have taken place on 7 June 1515.[16]

Staupitz claims in his last letter to Luther that he has himself been influenced by Luther's teaching,[17] even though he quickly adds some points at which he is aware of disagreements between them.[18] If Staupitz is correct in this self-estimate and is not merely responding in his usual diplomatic fashion to Luther's praise of his role in the early formation of evangelical theology, this fact serves only to complicate the historian's effort to assess the evidence from 1512 to 1524. Agreements between the two men cannot simply be regarded as prima facie evidence of the influence of Staupitz on Luther. Indeed, the reverse may be true. In certain cases Luther may be the teacher and Staupitz the disciple.

In addition to these specific difficulties which dog the footsteps of the

15. There are, of course, later accounts by Melanchthon, Mathesius, and Drescher, but they are clearly dependent on Luther for their information.
16. Scheel, *Luther*, 2:199. Cf. *WATR* 1, Nr. 137 (between 30 Nov. and 14 Dec. 1531).
17. In this letter Staupitz refers to himself as *discipulus tuus*. The letter is reprinted in Th. Kolde, *Die deutsche Augustiner-Congregation und Johann von Staupitz* (Gotha, 1879), pp. 446–47.
18. The disagreements center on *adiaphora* and on what Staupitz regards as an abuse of Christian freedom. Cf. Kolde, *Augustiner-Congregation*, p. 447.

historian who struggles to explain the relationship between Staupitz and Luther, there are other, more universal problems which he must face up to as well. What kind of evidence, after all, is required to establish influence? It is an exceedingly complex question and one which would deflect us from our main purpose were we to explore it in any depth.

Nevertheless, there are two principles which we need to fix firmly in mind before we survey the literature on the question of the relationship of Staupitz and Luther. Both principles are negative. A historian has not demonstrated influence when he has proven similarities in thought. If two people are found to teach the same thing or very nearly the same thing, it does not, in and of itself, prove the influence of one person upon the other. They may each have been influenced by a third party, who may or may not have been the same person in both cases. Or they may have, by very different paths and for very different reasons and under very different circumstances, come to similar conclusions. It is an important discovery when a historian can demonstrate similarities in thought between two theologians, who, he suspects, may have influenced each other. But similarities do not establish influence; they only establish agreement. That is important but it is not the same thing as influence. More and other evidence is required to establish influence.

Secondly, influence is not a synonym for agreement. Theological opponents may have a profound influence on each other. Just as the reading of Hume awoke Kant from his dogmatic slumbers, so, too, theologians who sharply disagree may find at the end of the day that they have more profoundly influenced each other than either would have thought possible at the time.

Similarly, theological statements may be heard and understood in ways not originally intended when they were uttered. Superficial agreements may cover subtle disagreements at a deeper level. Nevertheless, those hidden disagreements do not disprove influence any more than obvious agreements prove it. The question of agreement and disagreement, however important, is not the same question as the question of influence and a historian serves his audience badly when he confuses them.

To put the matter concretely, Luther and Staupitz may agree without having exercised the slightest influence on each other; they may disagree, either overtly or covertly, but do so as the result of a complex interaction and mutual influence. The historian must thread his way carefully through the sources and not claim too swiftly that organic similarities prove kinship. Caution, if not outright timidity, is the historian's best friend when the subject is influence.

In intellectual development there is such a thing as a *kairos*, the absolutely right moment for an idea to appear, an idea which under other circumstances might seem commonplace or banal. Staupitz made an indelible impression upon Luther with, among other things, some quite ordinary pastoral advice which any confessor who knew his business might have given. The advice went home because Luther was ripe to receive it. I would not want to leave the impression that that is the whole story of their relationship (if it were, this book would not have been written), but it is certainly a key element in it.

When Luther met Staupitz for the first time, Staupitz was in his forties.[19] He had been prior of the Augustinian cloister in Tübingen and was now vicar general of the Augustinian Observants. He was a skilled administrator with all the right connections in the Church and in the petty courts of Saxony. He was cool and polished with a good, if understated, sense of humor, free of the hyperbole and barnyard vulgarity which marked rougher peasant humor. He showed a decided preference for biblical and patristic arguments over the quarrelsome distinctions of late scholasticism, though he was at home in Thomas and Giles and Gerson, as one might expect of a doctor of theology from the University of Tübingen. He was a pastor and practitioner with a practitioner's knowledge of the fine points of canon law. He was a doer rather than a detached scholar. The existential issues which touched the life of faith were the issues which concerned him. For the rest he was content to think and let think, a man of many parts, destined from the very first for high office in the Church, restless behind the lectern in a university classroom.

Luther, on the other hand, was in his twenties, a young man from a small town with few family connections that mattered, a little shy and very uncertain of himself.[20] Staupitz took an interest in this retiring, bookish young man who bombarded him in the confessional with trivial faults inflated by his scrupulous imagination into what he feared were "mortal" sins. Staupitz gave him absolution for his real sins, subjected him to a cold

19. For a brief biography of Staupitz see my *Reformers in the Wings* (Philadelphia: Fortress Press, 1971), pp. 18–29.
20. Karl Holl once observed: "Luther hat es von Haus aus schwerer gehabt als andere religiöse Führer, überhaupt zu einem Selbstgefühl und vollends zu einem religiösen Selbstgefühl zu gelangen." K. Holl, *Gesammelte Aufsätze zur Kirchengeschichte I: Luther* (Tübingen, 1921), p. 382.

but bracing shower of sound theology and common sense, and groomed him to be his own replacement in the chair of biblical studies at the University of Wittenberg. Under the circumstances it comes as no very great surprise that Staupitz made an unforgettable impression on Luther. It would have been far more remarkable if he had not.

ii. *Images of Staupitz in Recent Research*

Because of the importance of Staupitz for Luther studies, historians have suggested a wide variety of images to characterize his theology.[21] The image of Staupitz, however, which has dominated Reformation historiography since the first half of the twentieth century is the image presented by Ernst Wolf[22] in 1927 in his important book, *Staupitz und Luther*.[23] Wolf's monograph was the first historical essay to make use of the critical edition of Staupitz's early sermons on Job[24] as well as the large collection of unedited sermons preserved at Salzburg.

Wolf argued in very difficult German prose that Staupitz was a disciple of Giles of Rome, the official doctor of the Augustinian Order, not simply in his formal academic theology but even in his teaching about the spiritual life. Thomas Aquinas was important for Staupitz as well, though never as important as Giles. The role of Thomas and Giles in forming the backbone of Staupitz's early theology (they are not cited in his later works) meant for Wolf that Staupitz could best be described as a kind of strongly Augustinian Thomist. Of nominalist or even Scotist influence on Staupitz, Wolf found virtually no trace, nothing at any rate which could bear comparison with the heavy citations of Giles and Thomas.

21. For a survey of earlier literature on Staupitz see my *Misericordia Dei*, pp. 16–22.

22. For bibliographical data see supra, footnote 11.

23. For a detailed summary of Wolf's argument and a critique, see my *Misericordia Dei*, pp. 19–31.

24. Georg Buchwald and Ernst Wolf, eds., *Staupitz, Tübinger Predigten*, QFRG 8 (Leipzig, 1927). A further discussion of the relationship of Staupitz and Luther which moves within the limits to the question set by Wolf can be found in Reinhard Schwarz, *Vorgeschichte der reformatorischen Bußtheologie*, AKG 41 (Berlin, 1968). Though Schwarz does not discount the influence of Staupitz, he hardly regards it as decisive: "Dennoch wurde Luther weder als Ockhamist, noch als Anhänger der Devotio moderna, noch als monastischer Theologe, auch nicht als Vertreter einer bernhardinischen Frömmigkeit oder augustinischen Theologie zum Reformator. Zum Reformator wurde er als der Lehrer einer neuen Theologie, die in der inneren Auseinandersetzung mit den Traditionen beim Schriftstudium herangereift war." *Vorgeschichte*, p. 297.

This supposed Thomistic orientation of Staupitz stood in sharp contrast to the training of Luther by the Erfurt nominalists in the theology of Ockham, Biel, and d'Ailly. Luther was not exposed in any significant degree to theThomistic vision of the world as a harmonious organism guided to its final end by a wise and intelligible providence. He had been taught, rather, to regard God as a despotic prince who governed the world by whim and caprice, who owed no one an explanation for his actions, and who looked at times suspiciously like a cosmic bully. Staupitz offered Luther a theological antidote to nominalist thought in the modified Thomism of Giles of Rome. While he did not convert Luther to Thomism, he did help him find consolation when his scrupulous conscience was battered with nagging doubts about his own election or driven to despair by the ambiguity of his own motives for wanting to serve God.

More important yet was Staupitz's success in correcting Luther's erroneous ideas about the nature of true penance. Luther had been taught that penance culminates in the love of God as the penitent, straining his natural moral capacities to their limit, suddenly achieves the disinterested love of God and neighbor commanded in the Law. God gives his grace, so ran the nominalist theory, to every penitent who loves God more than he loves anything else in the world.

Staupitz taught Luther that penance begins with the love of God rather than ends with it, that only those who have begun to love God can ever be distressed by their own sin or want to be separated from it by priestly absolution. Love of God is a gift which starts the process of repentance rather than an achievement which crowns it. When Luther grasped that idea, he was immeasurably consoled by it and stimulated to examine for himself all those passages in the Bible which dealt with "righteousness" and "repentance" and which he had always been careful to avoid for fear they might distress him further.

In my own book *Misericordia Dei*, published in 1968, I differed with Wolf's characterization of Staupitz as a Thomist. The non-Thomistic elements in Staupitz's thought were too important to his way of thinking about theological problems to permit him to be classified absent-mindedly as one more late medieval Thomist. When Staupitz emphasized the primacy of uncreated grace, quoted Gerson on the acceptation of works, or stressed the covenantal relationship of God to the world, he was talking in ways uncongenial to Thomas but congenial to the "Franciscan" orientation of the theological faculty at Tübingen. Staupitz was not a nominalist, certainly not in his doctrine of grace, where he was more one-sidedly Augustinian than Thomas himself, but he was not a Thomist either.[25] He was too sympathetic to motifs in nominalist theology, too rock-ribbed in his conservative Augustinianism, to be listed with Cajetan or even Capreolus. Whatever else Staupitz may have been for Luther, he was not Luther's tenuous link to the world of late medieval Thomism.

If Staupitz was not a Thomist, was he a radical Augustinian? The question is prompted by the fact that when Staupitz took his vows in the Augustinian cloister in Munich, he entered an order dedicated to theological study, especially to the study of the writings of St. Augustine (whom the Augustinians claimed to be the founder of their order). At Oxford, Cambridge, and Paris—but especially at Paris[26]—doctors of the

25. I was therefore a little surprised that the editors of the critical edition of Staupitz's *Libellus* have characterized my first book as ". . . der Versuch, den Lehrer nun umgekehrt statt in eine 'thomistisch-ägidianische' Lehrrichtung in eine 'skotistisch-nominalistische' einzuordnen." Johann von Staupitz, *Sämtliche Schriften; Abhandlungen, Predigten, Zeugnisse 2: Lateinische Schriften II*, ed. Lothar Graf zu Dohna, Richard Wetzel et al. (Berlin and New York: Walter De Gruyter, 1979), pp. 14–15. I argued at the time for the influence of Gerson and Biel, not the non-influence of Thomas and Giles. This is, of course, a question which can never be settled by merely listing and counting up the authorities cited by a medieval author. John Ruchrath of Wesel, who is, for what seem good reasons, always numbered among the adherents of the *via moderna*, never cites William Ockham. The doctor he cites most frequently is Thomas Aquinas and then, less frequently, Duns Scotus, the Victorines, Alexander of Hales, Bonaventura, Durandus, and Peter Auriole. He scarcely cites nominalist theologians at all. On this question see Erich Kleineidam, *Universitas Studii Erffordensis, Überblick über die Geschichte der Universität Erfurt im Mittelalter 1392–1521, Teil II: 1460–1521*, Erfurter Theologische Studien 22 (Leipzig, 1969), p. 22. Similarly Albert Lang argued in 1937 that Henry Totting of Oyta followed Ockham in philosophy and Thomas in theology. See A. Lang, *Heinrich Totting von Oyta* (Münster, 1937). Even Gabriel Biel, whose devotion to Ockham is not seriously in dispute, can quote Thomas Aquinas 236 times in Book IV of his *Collectorium* as against 41 quotations from Ockham. See Wilhelm Ernst, *Gott und Mensch am Vorabend der Reformation*, Erfurter Theologische Studien 28 (Leipzig, 1972), p. 93. For the relationship of Biel to Thomas Aquinas see the important unpublished dissertation by John L. Farthing, *Post Thomam* (Duke University, 1978). Staupitz can, of course, indicate strong agreement with Giles of Rome and Thomas Aquinas; e.g., on the question why Satan *sit perpetue irrevocabilis ad penitenciam*. Hiob (1497–98) 12.113.3–7. On the other hand, he can—as in 12.102.22–30—place some distance between himself and Thomas. He speaks of *sui [Thomas] adherentes et sequentes* as though he is not one of them. While he judges that the Thomistic opinion on a subject is buttressed *fortibus racionibus*, still he does not take a stand on the issue himself, but moves to the common ground between Thomas and his opponents. What is affirmed by all is what Staupitz wishes to affirm. Furthermore, in a disagreement between Thomas and Giles, Staupitz refuses to decide between them. 12.102.34–37.

26. Of the Augustinians whose commentaries on the *Sentences* have survived, forty-two out of seventy-five lectured on the *Sentences* at Paris, including such famous doctors as Giles of Rome, James of Viterbo, Alexander of San Elpidio, Henry of

Augustinian Order had distinguished themselves by the breadth and profundity of their learning.

Thomas Aquinas had no more famous pupil than Giles of Rome, who was so gifted and so blessed with independent insight that he was even regarded by some Thomists as a serious rival of Thomas.[27] Petrarch found in the Augustine scholarship of the Italian Augustinians an aid for his own studies in the writings of St. Augustine.[28] And there is probably, among the late medieval scholastics, no doctor whose mastery of the theology of St. Augustine is more impressive[29] or whose ability to interpret the ideas of St. Augustine in the categories of his own time is more successful[30] than the famous general of the Augustinian Order, Gregory of Rimini.

The question of the relationship of Staupitz to the theological traditions of his own order, to which he was exposed in a greater or lesser degree, and the role which those traditions played in the relationship of Staupitz to Luther, has remained one of the interesting, if unsolved, problems of Luther research. Was there a revival of Augustinianism in the Augustinian Order, which exercised an important influence through Staupitz on the

---

Friemar the elder, Augustinus of Ancona, William of Cremona, Henry of Friemar the younger, Hermann of Schildesche, Thomas of Strassburg, Gregory of Rimini, Alfons Vargas of Toledo, Hugolino of Orvieto, and Dionysius of Montina. Cf. the table found on pages 174–76 of Adolar Zumkeller, "Die Augustinerschule des Mittelalters: Vertreter und philosophisch-theologische Lehre," *Analecta Augustiniana* 27 (1964): 167–262.

27. "Dafür spricht auch der Umstand, daß manche Thomasschüler seiner Zeit in ihm [Giles of Rome] einen ausgesprochenen Gegner des Aquinaten sehen wollen." A. Zumkeller, "Augustinerschule," p. 180.

28. "Without wishing to make of this connection more than the evidence can sustain, it does not seem likely that Petrarch could have been unaware of the Augustinians' theological views, especially since he was introduced to the study of St. Augustine by the Augustinian Hermit, Dionigi of Borgo San Sepolcro." Charles Trinkaus, *In Our Image and Likeness: Humanity and Divinity in Italian Humanist Thought* (London: Constable, 1970), p. 61. Cf. A. Zumkeller, "Augustinerschule," pp. 206–7.

29. "What is so new in Gregory is the fact that he is the best Augustine scholar of the Middle Ages from the milieu which created the Milleloquium." Damasus Trapp, "Augustinian Theology of the 14th Century: Notes on Editions, Marginalia, Opinions and Book-Lore," *Augustiniana* 6 (1956): 181.

30. Gordon Leff, *Gregory of Rimini: Tradition and Innovation in Fourteenth Century Thought* (Manchester: The University Press, 1961), p. 241–42: ". . . what the Augustinians did for tradition in the thirteenth century he achieved in the fourteenth. He recast it and adapted it; and thereby preserved it. When the full history of fourteenth-century thought comes finally to be written, Gregory may well prove to have been its St. Bonaventure: the very divergence between them is the measure of his achievement."

theological development of the young Luther? As straightforward and simple as this question appears, it has proven unbelievably complex and difficult to answer.

III. *The Question of a Late Medieval Augustinian School*

What, for example, is meant by the term "Augustinian"? There are, so far as I am able to determine, five different senses in which this term is used by historians who discuss the phenomenon of late medieval Augustinianism. Apart from the sheer confusion this plurality of meanings introduces, there is the additional danger that a historian who has demonstrated the Augustinianism of a late medieval theologian in sense three will assume that he has proven in it senses two, four, and five as well; and, what is worse, will begin to draw conclusions on the basis of those unproven assumptions.

The term "Augustinian" may be used simply to designate the theology of the Latin West in general. No Latin theologian, however Pelagian his own theological instincts, is absolutely unaffected by the teaching of St. Augustine. If he finds little that is relevant for his theological situation in the anti-Pelagian writings of St. Augustine, he nevertheless may draw on the early anti-Manichaean writings in support of his own position. If he rejects with a shudder the Augustinian teaching concerning predestination, he may affirm with real gusto Augustinian ecclesiology. No Donatist rides against the enemy with the banner of a discredited heretic flying overhead. The teaching of St. Augustine's opponents is far more likely to be introduced under the aegis of an Augustine, now at last authentically understood. And one can always appeal to the moderate Augustine against the Augustine who spoke excessively.

It seems to me a serious mistake to regard as nothing more than theological posturing this universal respect for the teaching of St. Augustine, even when that teaching is misunderstood or abandoned. One can venerate St. Paul and yet come to very different conclusions about the import of his teaching. A medieval theologian may be genuine in his personal commitment to Augustine and still, for a variety of historical reasons beyond his own taste and preference, be insensitive to central themes in Augustine's thought. What is at stake is not his sincerity but the climate of the age in which he lives. When Thomas Aquinas meets Augustine, he changes him into an Aristotelian; when Martin Luther meets him, he transforms him into a *modernus*. It is the strength of the Augustinian tradition that it can speak with many tongues and is attractive even in a stunted or truncated form.

The term "Augustinian" may also be used to describe the theology of the Augustinian Order. When it is used in this sense, it is not used evaluatively to mean agreement with the teachings of St. Augustine, but descriptively to mean the actual teachings of members of the Augustinian Order, whether those teachings are faithful to St. Augustine or not. Adolar Zumkeller[31] and to some extent Damasus Trapp as well have used "Augustinian" in this somewhat more theologically neutral and descriptive sense. Are there any tendencies in the teaching of the Augustinian Order which characterize the order as a whole rather than a limited party within the order? If so, those tendencies deserve to be called Augustinian, as similar tendencies within the other mendicant orders might be called Franciscan or Dominican.

"Augustinian" may also be used evaluatively to describe a party within the Augustinian Order which agrees with St. Augustine on a wide range of disputed issues and at a depth which is more profound than the merely nominal Augustinianism common to all medieval theologians. A. V. Mueller is certainly using Augustinian in this sense when he attempts to show the continuity between the teaching of Hugolino of Orvieto, Simon Fidati of Cassia, Augustinus Favaroni of Rome, Jacobus Perez of Valencia, and Martin Luther.[32]

Some historians use the term "Augustinian" to describe the theological right wing of the later middle ages without paying any attention whatever to the affiliation of that right wing with one or another of the mendicant orders. If a theologian is Augustinian in a more radical sense than, say, Thomas Aquinas, he qualifies to be regarded as a late medieval Augustinian.[33] Perhaps right-wing is the wrong term to use, since it carries

31. For Zumkeller, "Augustinerschule" and "Ordensschule" are interchangeable terms. Cf. Zumkeller, "Augustinerschule," p. 169.

32. A. V. Mueller, *Luthers theologische Quellen* (Giessen, 1912); "Agostino Favaroni (1443) e la teologia di Lutero,"*Bilychnis* 3 (Rome, 1914), 373–87; "Giacomo Perez di Valenza, O.S. Aug., Vescovo di Chrysopoli e la teologia di Lutero," *Bilychnis* 9 (1920), 391–403; "Una fonte ignota del sistema di Lutero: Il beato Fidati da Cascia e la sua teologia," *Bilychnis* 10 (1921), fasc. 2.

33. I defended the use of Augustinian in this sense in my *Misericordia Dei*, pp. 30–34. Cf. my review of "Willigis Eckermann, OSA: *Gottschalk Hollen, OESA* (+1481): *Leben, Werke und Sakramentenlehre*," in ZKG 80 (1969), 411–14.

the connotation of opposition to all new theological currents of one's own time. Thomas Bradwardine could be said to be a right-wing Augustinian, who resisted and deplored the theological fashions of the fourteenth century, but hardly Gregory of Rimini, who gave Augustine a fourteenth-century voice.

Augustinian in this fourth sense is the designation for a sentiment in theology which takes Augustine without ice or water and which translates him into the theological vocabulary of one's own circle without dulling the bracing effect of his thought or deadening the ability of his formulations to jar one loose from one's own comfortable and commonplace way of thinking. In the later middle ages to be Augustinian in this sense generally meant that one embraced Augustine's less popular ideas on predestination or concupiscence or the impossibility of moral virtue without grace.

There is, of course, a fifth and last sense of the term "Augustinian" which also plays a part in adding complexity to the historian's task. As anyone who has studied theology knows, Augustinianism and Pelagianism are terms in the history of Christian thought with a life of their own. They are frequently used to mean not so much agreement with the teaching of Augustine and Pelagius in their original form as the embodiment of a theological tendency which in special cases may go beyond their original thinking. In one sense it is possible to say that Thomas Aquinas is more Augustinian than Luther on the question of merit, if the standard is fidelity to the original teaching of St. Augustine. But one can also hold, without taking an absurd and indefensible position, that Luther is more Augustinian than Thomas, if the frame of reference is the more perfect embodiment of a tendency. It all depends what you mean by "Augustinian."

To complicate the problem still further, historians must always bear in mind the context and intention of theological formulations. A theological proposition does not always mean the same thing in changed historical circumstances. Indeed, it may be necessary to formulate one's views in a more extreme way—or even in a totally different way—in order to say the same thing. Augustinians in the fifteenth century faced a revived semi-Pelagianism. Thomas Aquinas in the thirteenth century did not.[34] The fact of this difference of context between Thomas and fifteenth-century Augustinians

34. On this problem see Harry J. McSorley, *Luther: Right or Wrong?* (Minneapolis, 1969), p. 167.

has not been taken sufficiently into account by historians, who for the most part have been content merely to compare the formulations of these theologians against the standard of the teaching of St. Augustine.

IV. *Survey of Scholarship from Stange to Oberman*

Carl Stange in two essays published in 1900 and 1902 examined the relationship of Luther to the theology of his own order in general and to the theology of Gregory of Rimini in particular.[35] He argued that the theology of the middle ages could best be characterized as a theology of orders. The monastic vow implied, if it did not state explicitly, that the postulant would recognize the authority of the official doctors of his order. The monastic vow bound Dominicans to Thomas Aquinas and Albertus Magnus, Franciscans to Duns Scotus, and Augustinians to Giles of Rome and Gregory of Rimini.

Heinrich Hermelink countered Stange in 1906 in his dissertation on the theological faculty at Tübingen prior to the Reformation by arguing that medieval theology could be better characterized as a theology of universities than as a theology of orders.[36] In Cologne, Thomas and Albertus Magnus were regarded as authoritative, while Ockham reigned in Erfurt and Vienna. Consequently Dominicans at Cologne were *antiqui* and Dominicans at Erfurt and Vienna *moderni*.

This division can be clearly illustrated in the Augustinian Order. There the clash between Occamism and Thomism is perpetuated in the teaching of its two most prominent doctors, Gregory of Rimini and Giles of Rome. Staupitz relies on Giles, but Luther does not. Luther, on the other hand, praises Gregory of Rimini, who is never mentioned by Staupitz. This is a strange state of affairs if, indeed, the theology of orders takes precedence over the theology of universities.

Hermelink rejected the interpretation by Stange of the sentence of Jerome Dungersheim: "Egydius Rhomanus ordinis heremitarum s. Augustini, quem et Luther professus est." Stange had used the sentence to show Luther's commitment to the theology of his order in his monastic

---

35. Stange's essays are reprinted under the title, "Augustinischer Nominalismus," in Carl Stange, *Studien zur Theologie Luthers* (Gütersloh, 1928), 1:1–19.

36. For Hermelink's response to Stange see especially Heinrich Hermelink, *Die theologische Fakultät in Tübingen vor der Reformation, 1477–1534* (Stuttgart, 1906), pp. 95–96.

vow. This interpretation, however, rests on a misreading. The antecedent for the pronoun *quem* is *ordo* and not *Egydius Rhomanus*.

Luther did, of course, know the theology of Gregory of Rimini. According to the statutes of 1508 he was obligated to teach at Wittenberg according to the *via Gregorii*, which Hermelink regarded as nothing more than an approximate synonym for the *via Gabrielis*. At any rate, there is no evidence that Luther read Gregory or was familiar with the content of his theology until the time of the Leipzig disputation.[37] It is not possible to argue that Luther regarded himself as a Gregorian because of the wealth of evidence to the contrary. Of Ockham, Luther can say that he is ". . . scholasticorum doctorum sine dubio princeps et ingeniosissimus." It is, of course, possible that Luther has encountered some of Gregory's opinions through Gabriel Biel. Clearly, however, Luther was not directed to the study of Augustine by Gregory of Rimini. First Luther read Augustine and only at a later stage did he find confirmation of his views in the writings of Gregory of Rimini.

If there is no clear link between Staupitz, Luther, and Gregory of Rimini, there is a clear connection between Luther, Staupitz, and Gabriel Biel. Staupitz was a student of Steinbach and cites Biel in his first published work. Luther was trained in Biel's theology and even calls his students *mei Gabrielistae*. Luther is a disciple neither of Giles nor of Gregory. His most important teachers are not members of the Augustinian Order. Indeed, it may even have been the writings of Biel and not the atmosphere of the Augustinian Order which first awoke in Luther an interest in the study of St. Augustine. The important connections for Luther and Staupitz are not through the order but through the university.

The thesis that Luther was influenced by an Augustinian theological tradition within his own order was restated in a sharp and unsubtle way by

37. Leif Grane's studies tend to confirm this judgment of Hermelink against Stange and Zumkeller. In spite of the fact that Hugolino of Orvieto is in the library at Wittenberg, proof of the direct influence of Gregory on Luther is still lacking for the earliest period of Luther's development. "Doch nicht einmal unter dieser Voraussetzung kann gesagt werden, dass es bisher gelungen sei, Auswirkungen dieser Kenntnis von Gregor während der Jahre festzustellen, in denen die theologische Auffassung Luthers ausgeformt wurde. . . . Anderer Meinung ist A. Zumkeller. . . . Für seine Annahme, daß Luthers Kampf gegen den 'Pelagianismus' der Ockhamisten Anregung von Gregor erhalten hat, weist Zumkeller aber nur auf die Bemerkung über die Leipziger Disputation, *WA* 2,394 hin." Leif Grane, "Gregor von Rimini und Luthers Leipziger Disputation," *Studia Theologica* 22 (1968): 31. Heiko Oberman, on the other hand, feels a reasonably strong circumstantial case can be built for the earlier influence of Gregory on Luther. See H. A. Oberman, *Werden und Wertung der Reformation* (Tübingen, 1977), pp. 82–140.

Alphons Victor Mueller.[38] In a series of books and articles, beginning with *Luthers Theologische Quellen* in 1912, Mueller argued that Simon Fidati of Cassia (d.1348), Hugolino of Orvieto (d.1374), Augustinus Favaroni of Rome (d.1443), and Jacobus Perez of Valencia (d.1490) were representatives of an Augustinian school within the Augustinian Order and were in the most direct and immediate possible sense forerunners of the Reformation. Between their teaching and the new Reformation theology of Martin Luther there exists *una differenza di forma, non di sostanza.*

Mueller's thesis was, of course, discussed excitedly, both by Reformation historians and by specialists in late medieval thought. While Mueller did win some—at least partial—converts to his point of view, the great majority of historians were inclined to view his work with suspicion. There were, indeed, no strong prima facie grounds for confidence in his historical method. In his treatment of Perez and Luther, for example, Mueller summarized in only thirteen pages the teaching of Luther on faith, hope, certitude of salvation, penance, original sin, concupiscence, baptism, marriage, free will, and double justice, and compared Luther's teaching on each point with quotations from the writings of Perez. When on the last page Mueller triumphantly announced the full agreement of Luther and Perez, other historians might be forgiven if they preferred to reserve judgment.

The deficiencies in Mueller's methodology, the errors in his judgment, and the unnecessary sharpness of his reply to the historians who criticized him diminished the impact of his insights. Still there were some historians who were attracted to his ideas. In 1937 Eduard Stakemeier in his book *Der Kampf um Augustin auf dem Tridentinum* adopted part of Mueller's thesis. He agreed with the critics of Mueller that there existed an unbridgeable chasm between the teaching of the late medieval Augustinians and Martin Luther.[39] Nevertheless he saw in these late medieval friars forerunners of the Augustinian theologians at the Council of Trent.[40] Mueller's work, which was meant to cast light on Martin Luther, proved for

38. See supra, footnote 32.
39. Eduard Stakemeier, *Der Kampf um Augustin auf dem Tridentinum* (Paderborn, 1937), p. 21: "Zwischen diesen Augustinertheologen des 14. und 15. Jahrhunderts und der Gesamtlehre Martin Luthers ist ein solch wesentlicher und grundsätzlicher Unterschied, daß Müllers Aufstellungen in diesem Punkte unhaltbar sind. Was diese Augustiner über die Rechtfertigung aus dem Glauben sagen, ist nichts anderes als die schon vom hl. Thomas erklärte Lehre von der *fides formata iustificans.* Wenn Müller hier sagt, das sei nur *una differenza di forma, non di sostanza,* so widerspricht er sich selbst."
40. Stakemeier, *Kampf,* p. 22.

Stakemeier to cast light on the general of the Augustinian Order, Girolamo Seripando, instead.

Stakemeier's views were attacked by Hubert Jedin in a sharply critical article in the *Theologische Revue* for 1937.[41] Stakemeier had not proven the influence of these theologians on each other or on Seripando. He had simply placed the teaching of these theologians in parallel columns. He had demonstrated similarity, not influence. In order to prove the lines of influence, Stakemeier needed to do far more work in the primary sources, a very difficult task indeed since most of the materials needed to prove influence were still scattered and unedited! The need to pursue original research was made all the more pressing by the fact that in his book Stakemeier had not worked through the primary sources for himself, but had simply been content to repeat the evidence which Mueller had assembled in his own books and articles.

Jedin's judgment in his *History of the Council of Trent*, written many years later, summarizes fairly well the judgment of Catholic historians on Stakemeier's adaptation of Mueller: "Not proven, and scarcely capable of proof, is the hypothesis that Seripando was the most prominent upholder of a school tradition of his Order so that he and his fellow Augustinian Luther were as two branches on one and the same tree."[42]

The Protestant judgment concerning Mueller's original thesis was no less pessimistic. Gordon Rupp characterized the state of the question with these words: "The suggestion which A. V. Müller offered as the clue to Luther's development, that there was a revival of Augustinianism in the milieu in which Luther was trained, has never got beyond the stage of an interesting hypothesis. Augustine was always a main ingredient in medieval theology. The Bible and the Fathers, Augustine, Aristotle, were the main elements. You might add a double dose of Augustine to the preexisting mixture of Peter Lombard and Aristotle, but the result would be a Gregory of Rimini, or a Bradwardine, a recognizably mediaeval Augustinianism worlds apart from Luther's theology as it developed in these formative years."[43] And there, at least for the time being, the debate ground to a halt.

While interest in Mueller's thesis subsided, two related developments

41. *Theologische Revue* 36 (1937): 425–30.
42. Hubert Jedin, *A History of the Council of Trent, The First Sessions at Trent,* trans. Dom Ernest Graf, O.S.B. (Edinburgh, 1961), 2:258.
43. Gordon Rupp, *The Righteousness of God: Luther Studies* (London, 1953), p. 140.

provided the kind of evidence essential for a reassessment of the problem of a late medieval Augustinian school. On the one hand, a number of historians have, from a variety of different perspectives, written monographs and articles on individual theologians of the Augustinian Order: Schüler,[44] Würsdörfer,[45] Vignaux,[46] Oberman,[47] Trapp,[48] Leff,[49] and Eckermann[50] on Gregory of Rimini; Toner[51] on Augustinus Favaroni of Rome; Zumkeller on Hugolino of Orvieto,[52] Dionysius de Montina,[53] and Hermann von Schildesche;[54] Eckermann[55] on Gottschalk Hollen; Wolf,[56] Weijenborg,[57] Steinmetz,[58] and Oberman[59] on Staupitz; Stakemeier[60] and Jedin[61] on Seri-

44. Martin Schüler, *Prädestination, Sünde und Freiheit bei Gregor von Rimini* (Stuttgart, 1934).

45. J. Würsdörfer, *Erkennen und Wissen nach Gregor von Rimini*, BB, Vol. 20, Pt. 1 (Münster i.W., 1917).

46. Paul Vignaux, *Justification et prédestination au XIVe siècle, Duns Scot, Pierre d'Auriole, Guillaume d'Occam, Grégoire de Rimini* (Paris, 1934).

47. Heiko A. Oberman, *Archbishop Thomas Bradwardine: A Fourteenth Century Augustinian* (Utrecht, 1958); *The Harvest of Medieval Theology, Gabriel Biel and Late Medieval Nominalism* (Cambridge, Mass., 1963).

48. Supra, footnote 29.

49. Supra, footnote 30.

50. Willigis Eckermann, OSA, *Wort und Wirklichkeit, Das Sprachverständnis in der Theologie Gregors von Rimini und sein Weiterwirken in der Augustinerschule*, Cassiciacum 33 (Würzburg, 1978).

51. N. Toner, "The Doctrine of Original Sin According to Augustine of Rome (Favaroni) (+1443)," *Augustiniana* 7 (1957), 100–117, 349–66, 515–30; "The Doctrine of Justification According to Augustine of Rome (Favaroni) (+1443)," *Augustiniana* 8 (1958): 164–89, 299–327, 497–515.

52. Adolar Zumkeller, *Hugolin von Orvieto und seine theologische Erkenntnislehre* (Würzburg, 1941); "Hugolin von Orvieto (ob. 1373) über Urstand und Erbsünde," *Augustiniana* 3 (1953): 35–62, 165–93; 4 (1954); 25–46; "Hugolin von Orvieto über Prädestination, Rechtfertigung und Verdienst," *Augustiniana* 4 (1954): 109–56; 5 (1955): 5–51.

53. Adolar Zumkeller, *Dionysius de Montina: ein neuentdeckter Augustiner-theologe des Spätmittelalters* (Würzburg, 1948).

54. Adolar Zumkeller, *Hermann von Schildesche, O.E.S.A.* (Würzburg, 1957); *Schriftum und Lehre des Hermann von Schildesche* (Rome and Würzburg, 1959); "Wiedergefundene exegetische Werke Hermanns von Schildesche," *Augustinianum* 1 (1961): 236–72, 452–503; *Hermann von Schildesche, Tractatus Duo* (Würzburg, 1970).

55. Willigis Eckermann, OSA, *Gottschalk Hollen, OESA (+1481): Leben, Werke und Sakramentenlehre* (Würzburg, 1967).

56. Ernst Wolf, *Staupitz und Luther*, QFRG 9 (Leipzig, 1927); "Johann von Staupitz und die theologischen Anfänge Luthers," *Luther-Jahrbuch* 9 (1929): 43–86.

57. Reinoud Weijenborg, O.F.M., "Neuentdeckte Dokumente im Zusammenhang mit Luthers Romreise," *Antonianum* 32 (1957): 147–202.

58. David C. Steinmetz, *Misericordia Dei*, SMRT 4 (Leiden, 1968); *Reformers in the Wings* (Philadelphia, 1971): 18–29.

59. H. A. Oberman, *Werden und Wertung der Reformation* (Tübingen, 1977).

60. Eduard Stakemeier, *Der Kampf um Augustin auf dem Tridentinum* (Paderborn, 1937).

61. Hubert Jedin, *Girolamo Seripando*, 2 vols. (Würzburg, 1937).

pando; Werbeck[62] and Preus[63] on Jacobus Perez of Valencia; Lohse[64] and Ferdigg[65] on John of Paltz; O'Malley[66] on Giles of Viterbo—and so the list goes on. Though these books and articles do not represent a consensus on the nature of the theological currents in the Augustinian Order in the fourteenth and fifteenth centuries, they do provide us with the kind of data which were not generally available at the time when Mueller wrote his works.

The second development was equally important. Two historians, both members of the Augustinian Order, have attempted to elaborate an over-arching theory concerning the direction of the theological movement of the order as a whole. They have not presumed to single out a party within the order but simply to describe the common elements which united the separate parties. To use the distinctions I tried to draw at the beginning of this survey, they were not interested in isolating Augustinianism in senses three or four, as a radical party within or outside the Augustinian Order, but only in sense two, as the theology of the order itself, whether it agreed in all points with St. Augustine or not. The Augustinian school, as used by these historians, refers to the theology of the Augustinian Order as one might use the term Franciscan school to characterize the theology of that order. Nevertheless, it should be added that these his-torians came swiftly to the conclusion that the Augustinian Order does house a special kind of theological Augustinianism.

Damasus Trapp in his article, "Augustinian Theology of the 14th Cen-tury; Notes on Editions, Marginalia, Opinions and Book-Lore," divides Augustinian theology into two epochs.[67] The first stretches from Giles of Rome to Thomas of Strassburg; the second begins with Gregory of Rimini. Early Augustinianism is heavily influenced through Giles of

62. Wilfrid Werbeck, *Jacobus Perez von Valencia, Untersuchungen zu seinem Psalmenkommentar*, Beiträge zur historischen Theologie 28 (Tübingen, 1959).

63. James S. Preus, *From Shadow to Promise, Old Testament Interpretation from Augustine to the Young Luther* (Cambridge, Mass., 1969).

64. Bernhard Lohse, *Mönchtum und Reformation, Luthers Auseinandersetzung mit dem Mönchsideal des Mittelalters* (Göttingen, 1963).

65. Marcus Ferdigg, O.F.M., *De Vita et Operibus et Doctrina Joannis de Paltz, O.E.S.A.*, dissertation at the Antonianum (Rome, 1961). Since published in the *Analecta Augustiniana* 30 (1967): 210–321; 31 (1968): 155–318.

66. John W. O'Malley, S.J., *Giles of Viterbo on Church and Reform: A Study in Renaissance Thought*, SMRT 5 (Leiden, 1968); "Giles of Viterbo: A Sixteenth Century Text on Doctrinal Development," *Traditio* 22 (1966): 445–50; "Fulfillment of the Christian Golden Age under Pope Julius II: Text of a Discourse of Giles of Viterbo, 1507," *Traditio* 25 (1969): 265–338.

67. Damasus Trapp, O.E.S.A., "Augustinian Theology of the 14th Century: Notes on Editions, Marginalia, Opinions and Book-Lore," *Augustiniana* 6 (1956): 147–265.

Rome by Thomas Aquinas. It is not surprising, for example, that early Augustinians joined with Thomas Aquinas and the Dominicans in opposing the doctrine of the immaculate conception of the Virgin Mary defended by Scotus and the Franciscans. Later Augustinianism is more heavily dependent on Augustine himself, having recovered a far wider corpus of his writings than was available to Giles of Rome. As a sign of this new independence vis-a-vis its own past, the Augustinians shift their allegiance from the Dominicans to the Franciscans on the question of the immaculate conception. Throughout its history, however, Augustinianism is marked by its careful historical scholarship, by its desire for better texts and its concern for proper documentation. The Augustinian Order provides a home for intensive historical research in the writings of St. Augustine, a research which bears fruit in the theological reflections of its doctors.

A more ambitious attempt at synthesis than Trapp's important essay is the lengthy article by Adolar Zumkeller, "Die Augustinerschule des Mittelalters: Vertreter und philosophisch-theologische Lehre," in the *Analecta Augustiniana* for 1964.[68] Zumkeller accepts Trapp's periodization of the theology of the Augustinian Order and his stress on the importance for the Augustinians of a critical historical method. Nevertheless, even before that historical consciousness is fully developed, the Augustinian Order shows "ein klar ausgeprägtes augustinisches Element,"[69] reflected in the independence of Giles of Rome from the teaching of his master, St. Thomas Aquinas. The historical consciousness which marks the modern Augustinian school, beginning with Gregory of Rimini, intensifies but does not initiate the Augustinianism of the Augustinian Order.

This common Augustinian element which binds together the Augustinianism of Giles of Rome with the Augustinianism of Gregory of Rimini, Zumkeller, following A. Trapè, characterizes as a stress on the primacy of love and on the primacy of grace.[70] The Augustinians stressed the primacy of love when they gave preference to the good over the true, to the will over the intellect. Augustinians called theology an affective science and identified "charity" as its goal. The subject of theology is God as *glorificator* and the essence of eternal blessedness is an experience more aptly described as an act of will than as an act of intellect.

68. Adolar Zumkeller, "Die Augustinerschule des Mittelalters: Vertreter und philosophisch-theologische Lehre," *Analecta Augustiniana* 27 (1964): 167–262; "Das Ungenügen der menschlichen Werke bei den deutschen Predigern des Spätmittelalters," *Zeitschrift für katholische Theologie* 81 (1959): 265–305.
69. Zumkeller, "Augustinerschule," p. 193.
70. Zumkeller, "Augustinerschule," p. 194.

A stress on the primacy of grace meant at the very least a tendency to attribute as much significance as possible to the divine initiative in redemption and as little as possible to the initiative and activity of human nature. The Augustinians came down heavily on predestination and human depravity. They denied that it was possible to merit first grace and insisted in the strongest possible way on the necessity of grace for morally good acts. When forced to make a choice, the Augustinians tended to stress "uncreated grace," the personal presence of the Holy Spirit, even though they did not surrender the idea of "created grace," an infused habit of love.

These motifs, which are present from the very first, are heightened in intensity, following the compilation of the *Milleloquium* and the theological activity of Gregory of Rimini. The Augustinians are strongly oriented toward Scripture and the Fathers and sense the importance of exact quotation in theological exposition. Though the Augustinians quote their own doctors and are conscious of a theological identity over against the other orders, they are marked more by their source studies in Augustine than by their loyalty to the opinions of Giles of Rome.

In an address to the Fourth International Congress for Luther Research entitled "Headwaters of the Reformation: *Initia Lutheri—Initia Reformationis*," Heiko Oberman attempted to apply the results of this research on late medieval Augustinianism to the question of Luther's early theological development and the relation of Staupitz and Luther.[71] Though Oberman made use of the research of Trapp and Zumkeller, he was interested, like Mueller, to show a line of influence within the Augustinian Order, beginning with Gregory of Rimini and culminating in the theology of Martin Luther. As the father of the modern Augustinian school, Gregory combines three elements: nominalism, which shapes "the prolegomena of the *schola moderna Augustiniana*" and thus secures "the bridge to the world of the senses, of science and of experienced reality";[72] humanism "as the quest for the *mens Augustini* by returning to the *fontes Augustini*";[73] and Augustinianism reflected in Gregory's single-minded stress on justification *sola gratia*.[74] All three elements—nominalism, humanism and Augustinianism—are mediated to Luther by a line (by no means

71. Heiko A. Oberman, "Headwaters of the Reformation: *Initia Lutheri—Initia Reformationis*," in *Luther and the Dawn of the Modern Era*, ed. H. A. Oberman (Leiden, 1974), pp. 40–88.
72. Oberman, "Headwaters," p. 84.   74. Oberman, "Headwaters," p. 84.
73. Oberman, "Headwaters," p. 84.

unbroken), which one can trace in his own order. This modern Augustinian school or *via Gregorii* is given a new direction by Luther and becomes the "true theology" (*vera theologia*) of the circle of theologians at the University of Wittenberg.[75]

When Luther was called to teach philosophical ethics on the faculty of arts in 1508, he was obliged by the statutes of the University of Wittenberg to teach according to the *via Gregorii*. Whereas earlier historians had tended to regard this requirement only as an obligation to teach according to the *via moderna*, Oberman wishes to see in it the obligation to teach according to the principles of the modern Augustinian school.[76] This means for Oberman far more than the requirement to teach nominalist philosophy. The *via Gregorii* embraces elements of humanism and theological Augustinianism as well.

The Augustinian line within the Augustinian Order which interests Oberman begins with Gregory of Rimini, the *Doctor authenticus*, whose teaching was propagated in the order by Dionysius of Montina and Hugolino of Orvieto.[77] In Augustinus Favaroni (d. 1443) Oberman finds an ecclesiology which is the "allegorical counterpart to the tropological *commercium admirabile* between Christ and the believer,"[78] which is

75. Oberman, "Headwaters," p. 88: "We have the optimal chance therefore to do justice to the *initia Lutheri* when we see his development and discoveries as those of the Augustinian monk finding and founding a new direction for the already established *via Gregorii*."
76. Oberman, "Headwaters," pp. 77, 79–82.
77. Oberman, "Headwaters," p. 88: "We can say, however, that already in the earliest documents Luther thinks and writes as if Favaroni, Gregory of Rimini, and James Pérez combine in constituting his working library. Above all, this tradition is personified in Johann von Staupitz, to whose impetus Luther felt so deeply indebted. Luther for his part was willing to attest to Staupitz's role as forerunner of the *vera theologia*. . . ."
78. Oberman, "Headwaters," p. 73. The text of Favaroni which Oberman cites here is also quoted by Zumkeller, "Augustinerschule," pp. 237–38, though the conclusions which Oberman draws concerning these texts advance beyond Zumkeller. The ecclesiology, however, in which Christ is so identified with the Church and with the individual Christian that Christ and the Christian can be equated is already in Augustine. Augustine says, for example, in the *Tractatus in Joannis Evangelium* XXI.8, *PL* 35.1568: "Ergo gratulemur et agamus gratias, non solum nos Christianos factos esse, sed Christum. Intelligitis, fratres, gratiam Dei super nos capitis? Admiramini, gaudete, Christus facti sumus. Si enim caput ille, nos membra; totus homo, ille et nos." See also *Tractatus in Joannis Evangelium* XXVIII.1, *PL* 35.1622: "Non enim Christus in capite et non in corpore, sed Christus totus in capite et in corpore. Quod ergo membra ejus ipse: quod autem ipse, non continuo membra ejus." This ecclesiology becomes the basis for the happy exchange, which, as I shall show below, is also found in Augustine. It is true, however, that Augustine does not come to such a radical conclusion from his ecclesiology as "Christus quotidie peccat." But then

such a striking element of the treatise by Staupitz on predestination and which occurs roughly at the same time in Luther. The tradition of affective meditation, which is opposed to the speculative mysticism of Eckhart, is preserved for Luther by Jordan of Saxony, Ludolf of Saxony, and John of Palz.[79] Oberman even finds foreshadowings of Staupitz's reinterpretation of *gratia gratum faciens* (justifying grace) as the grace which makes God pleasing to the Christian in the sentence of Jordan of Saxony: "Omnia quae Christus passus est ita debent homini esse accepta et grata, ac si pro ipsius solummodo salute ea sit passus."[80]

According to Oberman, there are "at least four potential agents of transmission of the indicated Augustinian tradition":[81]

1. The library at Wittenberg had copies of both the *De gestis Salvatoris* by Simon Fidati of Cassia and a manuscript (the only known surviving copy) of the Sentences Commentary of Hugolino of Orvieto.[82] Since these books were accessible, Luther could have read them. And each in its own peculiar way represents elements of the *via Gregorii*, the modern Augustinian school.

2. It is possible that, during the years when Luther was writing his first lectures on the Psalms, he may have made use of the commentary on the Psalms by the Augustinian, Jacobus Perez of Valencia (d. 1490).[83] Perez agrees, as Wilfrid Werback has convincingly shown,[84] with Gregory of Rimini and his disciples on many questions.

3. In addition to Bartholomew von Usingen, Luther's teacher at Erfurt who stressed the importance of Gregory of Rimini,[85] John Staupitz was a particularly important channel of late medieval Augustinianism for Luther.[86] While Staupitz was, to use the language of Alfred Jeremias,[87] Luther's *Schüler* as well as his *Vater*, his decisive impact on Luther is be-

---

again neither does Staupitz, for whom the *commercium admirabile* is an important theme. I am inclined to agree with Favaroni when he claims an Augustinian basis for his theses in the writings of the bishop of Hippo, even though he draws some conclusions which Augustine does not draw.
79. Oberman, "Headwaters," p. 76.   83. Oberman, "Headwaters," p. 78.
80. Oberman, "Headwaters," p. 77.   84. Werbeck, *Perez*, pp. 210–58.
81. Oberman, "Headwaters," p. 78.   85. Oberman, "Headwaters," p. 80.
82. Oberman, "Headwaters," p. 78.   86. Oberman, "Headwaters," p. 78.
87. Note the title of the book: Alfred Jeremias, *Johannes von Staupitz, Luthers Vater und Schüler* (Berlin, 1926).

yond dispute. Luther claims that it was Staupitz who led him to the discovery of the meaning of real repentance (*vera penitentia*).[88] Furthermore, after the period of the Tübingen sermons, we find in the later Staupitz "the *acceptatio* doctrine as interpretation of the *sola gratia*, which he has combined with the tropological application of 'Favaroni's' theme of the exchange of *iustitia* and *peccata* between Christ and the believer."[89]

4. A fourth channel of possible influence was Andreas Bodenstein von Carlstadt. Carlstadt dedicates his commentary on the *De spiritu et littera* to Staupitz and indicates that Staupitz frees him from scholasticism "by showing the 'Christi dulcidinem' in the right relation of spirit and letter."[90] Carlstadt had lectured on Thomas Aquinas according to the principles of Capreolus. Since Capreolus saw as a major task the importance of bringing Gregory of Rimini and Thomas Aquinas into harmony with each other, he quotes long sections from Gregory in his *Defensiones*.[91] Thus by way of Carlstadt, Gregory of Rimini exercises an influence on the reform of theology at Wittenberg.

Oberman summarizes his position by observing: "Taking stock of this cumulative, admittedly circumstantial evidence, we can point to the *schola Augustiniana moderna*, initiated by Gregory of Rimini, reflected by Hugolin of Orvieto, apparently spiritually alive in the Erfurt Augustinian monastery, and transformed into a pastoral reform-theology by Staupitz, as the *occasio proxima*—not *causa!*—for the inception of the *theologia vera* at Wittenberg."[92]

In his most recent book, *Werden und Wertung der Reformation*, Oberman pushes his argument one step further by showing the pains which Wendelin Steinbach took in his lectures on Galatians and Hebrews to answer positions held by Gregory of Rimini. When one considers the institutional connection between Tübingen and Wittenberg and the personal connection between Steinbach and Staupitz, this concern with Gregory shows not only that he was known and used in the two universities but that Steinbach's reaction may even have been prompted by the stimulus which Gregory had provided for the reform of theology at Wittenberg.[93]

---

88. Oberman, "Headwaters," p. 78.
89. Oberman, "Headwaters," p. 78.
90. Oberman, "Headwaters," p. 79.
91. Oberman, "Headwaters," p. 79.
92. Oberman, "Headwaters," p. 82.
93. Oberman, *Werden und Wertung der Reformation*, pp. 131–32: "Festzuhalten ist, daß Gregor von Rimini in dieser Zeit nicht nur bekannt war, sondern auch als theologische Herausforderung ernstgenommen wurde und möglicherweise sogar in

By answering Gregory, Steinbach was implicitly criticizing a new movement in theology of which he did not wholly approve.

v. *Perspective of this Book*

The hypothesis that Staupitz is the mediator to Martin Luther of the *via
Gregorii*, the modern Augustinian school, presents the reader with several
difficulties. While Staupitz is in agreement with Gregory of Rimini on
many questions[94]—though he differs with him on several as well[95]—he
does not quote Gregory of Rimini, but repeatedly turns to Giles and
Thomas of Strassburg, representatives of the older Augustinian school.
To be sure, he does quote John of Paltz, but while John may be a representative of affective mysticism, he is hardly a radical Augustinian in his
theology. The strongest Augustinian opinions which Staupitz cites are
those of Augustine himself, supported, of course, by copious citations
from his famous disciple, Gregory the Great.

Merely to mention the name of John of Paltz is to show how prob-
lematical this reconstruction of the relationship of Staupitz and Luther is.
If there is an Augustinian tradition on grace which was embraced by the
entire order, why was Luther kept in ignorance of it at Erfurt?[96] Why
was it necessary for Staupitz to correct the theology which Luther had been
taught at Erfurt by members of his own order? And if Staupitz appealed
in conversation with Luther to a purer tradition of Augustinian theology
within their common order, why does Staupitz remain so reticent to cite
Gregory or Hugolino or Dionysius or Simon Fidati or Perez or Favaroni
in his published works?[97]

That is not to deny that Staupitz was influenced in his theological opin-

---

Reaktion auf die Anfänge der reformatorischen Theologie in Wittenberg zu einer
Antwort zwang."

94. For example, predestination *ante praevisa merita*, the dialectic of the *potentia
dei absoluta* and the *potentia dei ordinata*, the doctrine of *acceptatio divina* and the
denial of virtue apart from grace.

95. For example, reprobation *ante praevisa demerita*, all epistemological questions,
the rejection of *gratia creata*, the redefinition of *gratia gratum faciens*, and the identification of *prima gratia* with predestination.

96. Oberman does not claim that the *via Gregorii* is the tradition of the Augustinian Order as a whole and cites Paltz as an example of an Augustinian who is not
a follower of Gregory of Rimini. See Oberman, *Werden und Wertung der Reformation*, p. 131, footnote 172.

97. The fullest treatment of the sources which Staupitz quotes is found in Wolf,
Staupitz und Luther, pp. 23–25.

ions by the order of which he was a member. Staupitz is widely read in Augustine and in the sermons on Job quotes Augustine 163 times from 24 works.[98] He is attached to the opinions of Giles and Thomas Aquinas, though without becoming a Thomist.[99] When he differs with Thomas (and those differences are fundamental), he cites Jean Gerson[100] and not Gregory of Rimini as the supporting authority for his deviation. Except for his wide reading in Augustine and his partiality to certain nominalist ideas, Staupitz appears to be more of a representative of the older Augustinian school than of the school of Gregory of Rimini.

It is in his direct reliance on Augustine, whom he reads in the best texts which are available to him, that Staupitz is most faithful to the theological and historical impulses of his own order. Staupitz is no disciple of Gregory of Rimini, though he would cite him if he knew him better. He shares the humanists' distaste for the quarreling schools of the later middle ages and defies any attempt to fit him neatly into one of them.[101] The Bible and St. Augustine are all the school that Staupitz wants, though he reads them both, admittedly, in the context of the theological questions which were raised for him by the faculty of divinity at Tübingen.

This direct reliance on Augustine is obvious from the very beginning. Staupitz interprets the book of Job with the aid of the *Moralia* of Gregory the Great and the *Enarrationes in psalmos* of St. Augustine. In this Augustinian interpretation of the Old Testament Staupitz turns to Paul.[102] His sermons breathe the theological atmosphere of the Augustinian homiletical literature.

It is therefore not surprising that one can find in Augustine himself, especially in his sermons and commentaries on the Old Testament, many of the themes which are also distinctive of Staupitz's theology and which Oberman finds in Favaroni and Jordan of Saxony. It is possible that they

98. Wolf, *Staupitz und Luther*, p. 23.

99. For the relation of Staupitz to Giles of Rome and Thomas Aquinas, see Ernst Wolf, *Staupitz und Luther*, pp. 27–29, 80–82, 219–20. Wolf overestimated the importance of Thomas and Giles for Staupitz (on this point see my *Misericordia Dei*, pp. 22–28); nevertheless Staupitz does rely on them, especially in matters of epistemology.

100. Staupitz, *Hiob* (1497–98) 23.186.41–187.3. Cf. my *Misericordia Dei*, pp. 27, 106–7.

101. Luther reports that Staupitz frequently quoted the saying of Conrad Summenhart, "Quis liberabit me ab ista rixosa theologia?" *WATR* 5 Nr. 5374 (Summer 1540).

102. One can see this movement from Augustine on the Psalms to an interpretation of Pauline literature in specific cases as well as generally. In his eleventh sermon on Job, Staupitz moves from Augustine to Psalm 90 to an interpretation of Romans 8. Cf. *Hiob* 11.97.6ff.

are in all three because they are first in Augustine and their presence may not prove influence by the *via Gregorii* but only influence by a common source, the Augustine whose mind is the special concern of both the modern and the older Augustinian school. That Staupitz, Favaroni, and Jordan agree may in the last analysis be evidence that the historical scholarship of the Augustinian Order, the return *ad fontes Augustini,* may have issued in important theological conclusions.

To take only two examples of the way in which Staupitz may have been directly influenced by his study of Augustine, Augustine makes the point in his sermons that the property of man is his sin, untruth, and death.[103] The property of God is his goodness, truth, and life. The sinner with his property possesses God and is possessed by him. Christian experience may be summed up as this possession of God,[104] whom one possesses only as one renounces the title to oneself. What is properly God's (namely, life) becomes man's; and what is proper to human nature (namely, death) becomes God's.[105]

In other words, one finds already in Augustine's sermons on the New Testament the "marvelous exchange" (*commercium admirabile*) between Christ and the Christian of which both Luther and Staupitz make so much.[106] To be sure, the marriage metaphor[107] is not employed by Augustine as it is by Luther[108] and Staupitz[109] nor is the exchange an exchange of sin and righteousness but rather of death and life. Nevertheless, there is an exchange of properties between Christ and the Christian in which the Christian trades his mortality for the eternal life found in Christ. When Staupitz uses the idea of a heavenly exchange between Christ and the Christian, he may in fact be doing nothing more than adapting an important theme from the homiletical literature of St. Augustine.

In the same way Staupitz's reinterpretation of justifying grace (*gratia gratum faciens*) as the grace which makes God pleasing to the Christian

103. *Serm.* 32.10.10, PL 38.202; *In Ps.* 145.11, PL 37.1891.

104. *Serm.* 47.16.30, PL 38.315–16; *In Ps.* 145.11, PL 37.1891–92; *Serm.* 166.2.2, 3.3, PL 38.908–9.

105. *In Ps.* 30, En. 2.1.3–4, PL 36.230–32; *Serm.* 35.2–3, PL 38.213–14.

106. *Serm.* 80.5, PL 38.496.

107. Augustine can speak of the exchange taking place between the *sponsus* and *sponsa.* Cf. *In Ps.* 30, En. 2.1.4, PL 36.232. But the images of a business transaction and of an exchange between head and body are the more dominant images. For Luther and Staupitz the central image is the marriage metaphor.

108. H. A. Oberman, "'Iustitia Christi' and 'Iustitia Dei,' Luther and the Scholastic Doctrines of Justification," HTR 59 (1966), 1–26.

109. Cf. *Misericordia Dei,* pp. 90–91.

may be explained as a rather scholastic translation of the maxim developed by Augustine in his second discourse on Psalm 32 (33): "He pleases God who is pleased with God."[110] The mark of the justified person is that he takes pleasure in God. Because he is pleased with God, he praises him. And that praise is in its own turn pleasing to God.

The idea is, of course, central to Staupitz. Justification is the restoration of the ability to praise God.[111] Justified men and women praise God because they find God pleasing. The grace which restores this praise to the otherwise dumb lips of sinners is labeled by Staupitz as *gratia gratum faciens* ("grace which makes pleasing"), not because it makes the Christian pleasing to God, although that was the common medieval opinion, but because it renders God pleasing to the elect.

There may, obviously, be a much more complex history behind Staupitz's redefinition of *gratia gratum faciens* and he may, in fact, prove not to be the first medieval theologian to define it that way. However, since, as Ockham taught us, that theory is best which explains the evidence with the fewest assumptions, I am inclined to regard it as nothing more than a restatement of a maxim which was in Augustine all along, if only one had eyes to see it. It is evidence, not of Staupitz's interest in Jordan of Saxony (a thesis which is open to some question) but of his proven attachment to the *Enarrationes in psalmos* (a fact which is beyond debate).[112]

While it is important to place the encounter of Luther and Staupitz in the broadest possible context, there is a very real danger in all this talk of schools and traditions of losing the particular historical circumstances of their first meeting. They did not meet in the classroom or library, but in the chapel, the refectory, and the confessional. Luther met Staupitz as youth meets middle age, as a penitent meets his confessor, as a friar meets his superior, as the grandson of peasants meets a cultured Saxon nobleman, as a recent Master of Arts meets a learned Doctor of Divinity. Even before they met, Luther owed Staupitz obedience and respect, both as the

110. *In Ps.* 32, Second Discourse, Serm. 1.1, PL 36.277: "Et breve praeceptum est: Ille placet Deo, cui placet Deus."
111. Cf. *Misericordia Dei*, p. 55, for a brief résumé on this point. See also Augustine, *In Ps.* 44.9, PL 36.500: ". . . significare voluerit summum hominis opus non esse, nisi Deum laudare."
112. Erwin Iserloh is also of the opinion that Luther finds the "happy exchange" in the writings of St. Augustine, though he does not comment on the use of this image by Staupitz or of the possible role of Staupitz as a mediator of this tradition to Luther. Erwin Iserloh, "Luther und die Mystik," in *The Church, Mysticism, Sanctification and the Natural in Luther's Thought* (Philadelphia: Fortress Press, 1967), pp. 60–83, esp. 71–75.

vicar general of his order and as a doctor of the Church. While their first encounter blossomed into friendship, Luther was always quite specific in locating the crucial moments of that relationship in the confessional or in pastoral conversation relating to the confessional. Luther did not listen to a course of theological lectures by Staupitz or participate with him in a seminar on a biblical subject. Most of what Staupitz said to Luther that really mattered was protected by the seal of the confessional. If Luther had not revealed what took place in those conversations, we should never have heard about them at all.

While the ultimate end of penance was absolution from postbaptismal sin and the restoration of friendship with God, the sacrament also served the more proximate pastoral aims of discipline and consolation.[113] The discipline of the Church protected the penitent from presumption, while the consolation it offered kept him from despair. Luther attempted to derive consolation from the sacrament by rigorous adherence to its discipline, including the discipline of living in a perpetual state of satisfaction by reason of his monastic vow.[114] But the discipline which consoled most people well enough failed signally to console Luther.

When Luther came to Staupitz in despair, Staupitz had to find out as quickly as he could to what extent the problem was with Luther (and there can be little doubt that part of Luther's problem was neurotic guilt or what the medieval Church called "scruples")[115] and to what extent the problem was with what Luther had been taught to expect from the sacrament. Staupitz soon discovered both that Luther had to be adjusted to the sacrament and the sacrament reinterpreted to Luther.

The remarkable thing about Luther's memory of Staupitz's advice is its astonishing brevity. At most Luther recalls a sentence or two which struck him forcefully at the time and gave him the consolation which had

113. On this question see the excellent study by Thomas N. Tentler, *Sin and Confession on the Eve of the Reformation* (Princeton, N.J., 1977).

114. Otto Scheel has assembled most of the important memories of Staupitz in his *Dokumente zu Luthers Entwicklung*, second edition (Tübingen, 1929). Since it is useful to see Luther's memories of Staupitz together in one volume, I will give references to paragraphs in this volume, rather than in the Weimar edition. On Luther's search for consolation through rigorous discipline, see Scheel, *Dokumente*, 169, 265.

115. Tentler observes in *Sin and Confession*, p. 156, that the sense of sin inculcated in the faithful by penitential literature in the late Middle Ages verged always on scrupulosity: "Is the sense of sin taught in this literature simple scrupulosity? The answer, as usual, is yes and no. It is yes because of the sheer number and variety of sins, the implacable search into the mental life of the penitent and the relentless demand that he make up his mind about the gravity of an act and the degree of his consent. Know thyself becomes an exhausting activity."

eluded him in the sacrament. Never does he seem to remember any very complicated theological argument. One searches in vain through Luther's recollections for a lengthy discourse by Staupitz against Biel on free will or a hint which led Luther to an appreciative savoring of some particularly juicy passage in Gregory of Rimini or Jacobus Perez. The advice is brief, uncomplicated, and direct. But the simple advice untangled a web of complications in Luther's mind, partly of his own constructing, partly forced on him by a theology which begged too many of the really important questions.

Staupitz's advice as Luther remembered it was roughly of two kinds. There was the tough, hearty, no-nonsense, straightforward pastoral advice which any good pastor would have given to a penitent tormented by excessive scruples. Biel might have given it himself or Steinbach. Biel and Staupitz would have given the same advice for very different theological reasons, but the differences in theology do not, so far as I can tell, enter into the picture at all. Luther is not so much impressed with the theological foundations of this advice as with the advice itself. And in itself the advice is unremarkable. Who said it and under what circumstances were fully as important to Luther as what was said.

When Staupitz urged on Luther the usefulness of his temptations[116] (though Luther was aware at the time of a difference between the sense in which Staupitz was offering the advice and the sense in which he could accept it),[117] when he pointed Luther to the crucified Christ in the midst of his anxieties over election,[118] and when he warned him of the dangers of a scrupulous conscience,[119] he was giving sound but wholly traditional advice. Even his strategy for dealing with Luther's scruples was taken directly from the best manuals of pastoral care.

The worst thing a pastor could do with a scrupulous penitent was cater to him, nurse along his neurotic guilt, protect him from confrontation with the fact that his refusal to believe in God's mercy was a dangerous and potentially fatal sin.[120] If our thoughts condemn us, our thoughts are not Christ.[121] Our anger with God is not the same thing as God's anger with

116. Scheel, Dokumente, 138, 207, 209, 210.
117. Scheel, Dokumente, 199, 273.
118. Scheel, Dokumente, 225, 256, 262, 274, 456.
119. Scheel, Dokumente, 201, 209.
120. Tentler, Sin and Confession, p. 76: "For the most part, as we shall see later, scrupulosity was treated gently. But at times an author could deal with it for what it was supposed to be—a serious spiritual vice—and take a harder line."
121. Scheel, Dokumente, 201.

us.[122] There is, of course, such a thing as the wrath of God and it is to be feared. But the wrath of God never falls on even the weakest penitent who clings simply to the cross of Christ.

When Luther tried to confess faults that were not sins, Staupitz accused him of parading toy sins before God and of confusing social indiscretions with moral transgressions.[123] When Luther was inclined to mope and indulge in a morbid introspection of his conscience, Staupitz set him to work studying for his theological doctorate.[124] The study of theology might make clear to Luther that while God is merciful to real sinners, imaginary sinners remain trapped in illusions spun out of their own fears. Staupitz was convinced that soft handling would never teach Luther the difference between real sin and entirely unjustified feelings of guilt. Luther had to learn that it was not a sign of great piety to mistrust the mercy of God but of stupid, obstinate, and wholly unnecessary unbelief. Clinging to God's "No" when one should celebrate God's "Yes" in the gospel was the worst kind of unbelief.

But not all of Staupitz's advice comes under the heading of sound, commonsense, Johnsonian *pastoralia*. Staupitz had also to exercise his office as a doctor of the Church and correct Luther's theology at several points where he had been misled by the nominalist orientation of his Erfurt teachers. Staupitz was in a particularly good position to do this, because his own experience as a student in Tübingen had taught him exactly what were the dangerous tendencies in German nominalist thought, the aberrations which could never be reconciled with Pauline theology or with Augustine.

Staupitz made three observations about theology proper which Luther found particularly helpful. He taught Luther that penance begins with the love of God, even though Luther had been given to understand that the love of God is the final step in a process of self-discipline and the assumption of rigorous responsibility for one's status in the presence of God.[125] He warned Luther of the danger of trusting in one's own natural moral energies, even though Luther had learned that it was precisely by relying on those same natural powers that one could merit the favor of God.[126] And he gave Luther a rough and ready principle of verifiability

122. Scheel, Dokumente, 209.
123. Scheel, Dokumente, 487.
124. Scheel, Dokumente, 5, 174, 230, 304, 399, 409, 444, 472, 485.
125. Scheel, Dokumente, 18.
126. Scheel, Dokumente, 166, 170, 195, 264, 486.

for any system of doctrine: that theology is true which gives glory to God rather than to men.[127] Staupitz intended it as a principle which would exclude nominalist theologies of grace, though Luther cited it much later in life as a justification for Protestant theories of salvation over against traditional Catholic. In all these principles it was important that Staupitz was an Augustinian rather than a nominalist. While Biel might have given the general pastoral advice which Staupitz had given, he would have found himself at loggerheads with Staupitz over these three theological propositions.

The fact that Staupitz corrects Luther's theology and that Luther cites one of these corrections as fundamental to his new understanding of justification raises the interesting and important question whether for a period of time—at least, say, from 1509 to 1518—Luther should be understood primarily as a disciple of John Staupitz. Did Luther, in other words, criticize German nominalism from the perspective of his old confessor and patron? Did he abandon that perspective sometime after 1517 when a combination of external pressures and internal stimuli led him to take the irrevocable step across the gulf which separates late medieval Augustinianism from the newer and more radical theology of early Protestantism? Or was Luther from the very beginning a new and original thinker, who was, to be sure, inspired by Staupitz, corrected by him, steadied by his more mature and sensible approach to theological issues, but as free and independent in his positions as any thinker can be who is deeply indebted to others?

It is not an easy question to answer and it has never been answered to anyone's complete satisfaction. This book will try to answer the question insofar as the documentary evidence will support such an answer. In order to do so, it will be necessary to examine in detail four related problems: to what extent was the young Luther dependent on Staupitz in his approach to biblical studies, in his doctrine of justification, in his understanding of the mind of Paul, and in his redefinition of religious ecstasy? The resolution of those problems will occupy us for the next four chapters.

127. Scheel, *Dokumente*, 161.

II. HERMENEUTIC AND OLD TESTAMENT INTERPRETATION

The question whether Luther in his first lectures on the Psalms was following an approach to the interpretation of the Bible initiated by Staupitz is not a new one. Karl Bauer in his famous book, *Die Wittenberger Universitätstheologie und die Anfänge der deutschen Reformation*, suggested something of the sort. According to Bauer, Luther became a reformer through the discovery and application of a new hermeneutic.[1] Since the crucial period for the development of this hermeneutical theory was 1516 to 1519, the new hermeneutic in its fully developed form cannot be found in the earlier *Dictata super Psalterium* (1513–15).[2]

That disappointing conclusion ought to have ruled out by itself all possibility of the influence of Staupitz, were it not for the immediate qualification which Bauer added. While Luther's earliest exegetical writings are not guided by the interpretive principles which mark his mature biblical studies, they do contain the roots of his new hermeneutic. By "roots" Bauer meant a preoccupation with the Christological center[3] of Scripture and a tendency to direct all exegesis toward the practical religious concerns of the individual.[4] These rudimentary elements, these building blocks of Luther's later hermeneutical theory, were derived, so far as Bauer could see, from Staupitz.[5] There was, then, a brief period, roughly from 1513 to 1515, when Luther interpreted Scripture under the decisive influence of Staupitz. Unfortunately, Bauer did not provide adequate documentation for this stimulating hypothesis and it has remained nothing more than an obiter dictum.

1. Karl Bauer, *Die Wittenberger Universitätstheologie und die Anfänge der deutschen Reformation* (Tübingen, 1928), p. 145: "Aber zum Reformator ist er [Luther] weder durch seinen Nominalismus, noch durch die Anregungen, die ihm vom Humanismus kamen, sondern durch seine neue Hermeneutik."
2. Bauer, *Wittenberger Universitätstheologie*, p. 147: "Die Zeit der ersten Psalmenvorlesung verrät noch nichts von dem künftigen Reformator."
3. Bauer, *Wittenberger Universitätstheologie*, p. 22: "Gerade damit aber, daß Staupitz auf Christus hinwies, hatte er den leitenden Gesichtspunkt gewonnen, der dann auch bei Luther wiederkehrt."
4. Bauer, *Wittenberger Universitätstheologie*, p. 145: "Auf dem biblischen Lehrstuhl der Wittenberger Hochschule setzte er die hermeneutischen Traditionen seines Vorgängers Staupitz fort. Auf die *practica* der Bibel kam es ihm an. Er hörte aus ihr die Botschaft an jeden Christenmenschen heraus: *Tua res agitur!*"
5. Bauer, *Wittenberger Universitätstheologie*, p. 21: "Der Meister, von welchem Luther auch für seine Hermeneutik am meisten gelernt hat, ist Staupitz."

Karl Holl differed with Bauer, at least over Bauer's late dating of the new hermeneutic.[6] Already in the lectures on the Psalms there were signs of a new approach to Scripture. Together with other historians such as Hirsch,[7] Vogelsang,[8] and Seeberg,[9] Holl managed to clarify the centrality of the tropological sense of Scripture for the young Luther[10] and to demonstrate that an important relationship exists between Luther's hermeneutic and his developing theory of justification by faith.

In 1951 Gerhard Ebeling asserted in an essay in the *Zeitschrift für Theologie und Kirche*[11] that Bauer had been corrected by subsequent research but not contradicted by it.[12] Luther's new hermeneutic took shape, as Bauer had originally argued, in the period from 1516 to 1519. Still that new hermeneutic was preceded by an earlier hermeneutical shift already evident in the *Dictata super Psalterium*.[13] The years 1513 to 1515 mark an intermediate period in Luther's theological development. During this time he broke with the old medieval approach to Scripture and laid the foundation for the new approach to the text which he constructed after 1516.

While scholars have examined in some detail Bauer's first hypothesis concerning the importance of a new hermeneutic for Luther's development as a Protestant Reformer,[14] relatively scant attention has been paid by them

6. Karl Holl, "Luthers Bedeutung für den Fortschritt der Auslegungskunst," in *Gesammelte Aufsätze zur Kirchengeschichte I, Luther* (Tübingen, 1932), pp. 544–82, especially pp. 545–50.

7. Emanuel Hirsch, "Initium theologiae Lutheri," in *Lutherstudien II* (Gütersloh, 1954), pp. 9–35, especially pp. 33–35.

8. Erich Vogelsang, *Die Anfänge von Luthers Christologie nach der ersten Psalmenvorlesung*, AKG 15 (Berlin and Leipzig, 1929). See especially pp. 16–30 and 40–61.

9. Erich Seeberg, "Die Anfänge der Theologie Luthers," ZKG 53 (1934), 229–41; *Luthers Theologie*, Vol. 2 (Göttingen, 1937).

10. Holl argued that what Luther means by the tropological sense of Scripture is "nicht einzelne zufällig herausgegriffene sittliche Weisungen, wie man sie nach jeweiligem Bedünken an den Text anschließen mochte, sondern etwas Einheitliches, scharf Umrissenes, immer wieder von ihm Eingeschärftes. Es ist kurz gesagt das Paulinische Evangelium, was Luther als den tropologischen Sinn aus den Psalmen herausholt. . . ." *Gesammelte Aufsätze I*, p. 546.

11. Gerhard Ebeling, "Die Anfänge von Luthers Hermeneutik," ZThK 48 (1951): 172–230. The essay is reprinted in Gerhard Ebeling, *Lutherstudien I* (Tübingen, 1971), pp. 1–68. Citations are from the revised essay in the *Lutherstudien*.

12. Ebeling, *Lutherstudien I*, p. 6.

13. Ebeling, *Lutherstudien I*, p. 7.

14. Against the prevailing German scholarship James S. Preus argued in *From Shadow to Promise, Old Testament Interpretation from Augustine to the Young Luther* (Cambridge, Mass.: Harvard University Press, 1969) that the christological and tropological interpretation of the Psalms hindered rather than helped Luther to his discovery of justification by faith alone in the promise of God. There is a hermeneu-

to Bauer's second hypothesis concerning the decisive influence of Staupitz on Luther's new hermeneutical discoveries. Did Staupitz belong to the intermediate period of Luther's hermeneutical development or was he representative of the older medieval approach to the text which Luther swiftly left behind? Did Luther's appointment to the chair of Sacred Scripture at Wittenberg as the successor to John Staupitz guarantee, at least at first, a certain continuity in approach to the interpretation of the Bible?

Anyone who sets out to answer this question must labor under an irremediable handicap. None of Staupitz's university lectures on the Old Testament has survived.[15] All that has survived from the early period of Staupitz's theological career, aside from his *Decisio* of 1500 and occasional letters, is homiletical or pastoral in nature: manuscripts of sermons, reports of sermons recorded by others, and a German treatise, published in Leipzig and dedicated to the Countess of Mansfeld. While the German homilies focus on gospel lessons, the Latin sermons, clearly the most important theological statement from Staupitz until his *Libellus* of 1517, interpret Job 1:1–2:10.

By 1515 Luther, on the other hand, had delivered a lengthy series of lectures on all 150 psalms. The notebooks for those lectures have been preserved and contain marginal and interlinear glosses as well as more extended scholia.[16] Luther had also, by this time, preached numerous ser-

---

tical shift in Luther's first lectures on the Psalms as Luther recovers the *sensus propheticus* as the word of the Old Testament prophet to the faithful synagogue who lives by a faith which is really *exspectatio* or future hope grounded in the *testimonium* or promise of God. The Church should conform itself to the faithful synagogue and live by faith alone in the word of promise, a faith which like the hope of the faithful synagogue is future-oriented. This shift takes place at Psalm 118 [119]. Preus's argument has been challenged by Gordon Rupp in his review in the *JTS*, N.S. 23 (1972), 276–78 and more extensively by Scott Hendrix, *Ecclesia in Via, Ecclesiological Developments in the Medieval Psalms Exegesis and the Dictata Super Psalterium of Martin Luther*, SMRT 8 (Leiden: E. J. Brill, 1974), especially pp. 263–87. I find the arguments of Rupp and Hendrix convincing and cannot accept the thesis of Preus's otherwise interesting and useful book.

15. Bauer admits that Staupitz's biblical lectures at Wittenberg have not survived, but does not feel that this fact damages his thesis, since Luther did not hear them. "Luther hat seine hermeneutische Methode aus dem gelegentlich Gebrauch gelernt, den Staupitz ihm gegenüber im seelsorgerlichen Gespräche von einzelnen Schriftstellen machte." Bauer adds in a footnote, "So ist wohl der nicht ganz klare Satz: 'der hatt mir occasionen geben' zu verstehen." Bauer, *Wittenberger Universitätstheologie*, pp. 21–22.

16. In this connection see Gerhard Ebeling, "Luthers Psalterdruck vom Jahre 1513," in *Lutherstudien I*, pp. 69–131, and the "Vorläufige Einleitung" in WA 55¹.1, 15*–33*.

mons, mostly on gospel lessons, though no sustained series of sermons comparable to Staupitz's thirty-four sermons on Job. The most important material for comparison is, in other words, not absolutely comparable. Nevertheless enough material does exist, sufficiently comparable in nature, to make it possible to draw at least some tentative conclusions concerning similarities and differences in their method of biblical interpretation.

1. Staupitz as an Interpreter of Job

Throughout his lifetime Staupitz was in touch with representatives of German humanism.[17] As a student in Tübingen,[18] as a preacher in Nuremberg,[19] and as a professor in Wittenberg,[20] Staupitz numbered humanist

17. For a discussion of Staupitz's connections with German humanism, see Helmar Junghans, "Der Einfluß des Humanismus auf Luthers Entwicklung bis 1518," *Luther-Jahrbuch* 37 (1970): 37–101, especially pp. 86–101.

18. Heinrich Bebel, Conrad Summenhart, and Paul Scriptoris opposed the scholastic method at Tübingen. Bebel was Professor of Poetry and Rhetoric and interested in the development of a German literature as well as in the appreciation of the classics of the Latin poetic tradition. Summenhart, who was regarded as a humanist by Bebel and Wimpfeling, was a Hebraist of considerable ability. Together with Scriptoris he pressed for an intensive study of Scripture at the university. Whether Staupitz heard Bebel lecture is not known, but there is evidence for his contact with Scriptoris and Summenhart. Staupitz loved to cite the saying of Summenhart: "Quis liberabit me ab ista rixosa theologia?" The rejection of the quarrelsome methods of scholastic theology in favor of the study of Scripture was a strong point of German humanism. Staupitz's agreement with the humanist reform program brought him in touch with humanists throughout his life. Cf. Junghans, "Einfluß des Humanismus," pp. 86–87.

19. Many of the leading citizens of Nuremberg formed a society around Staupitz which they named in typical humanist fashion a *Sodalitas Staupitziana*. The sodality included such humanist figures as the legal scholar, Christoph Scheurl, and the important German humanist, Willibald Pirckheimer. Cf. Junghans, "Einfluß des Humanismus," pp. 87–88.

20. Junghans remarks that "die Abkehr von der scholastischen Lehrmethode und die Hinwendung zu verstärktem Bibelstudium und zu praktischer Frömmigkeit brachten von Staupitz wiederholt mit Humanisten in Berührung. Und es war wohl kein Zufall, daß unter den Männern, die von Staupitz für die Wittenberger Universität warb, auch Humanisten waren." Junghans, "Einfluß des Humanismus," p. 87. Junghans documents this contention (pp. 94–101) by listing the Wittenberg faculty members who had been or still were identified with humanism. The first rector, Dr. Martin Pollich of Mellerstadt, had strong connections with humanism in his youth and had used the writing of the Italian humanist, Nicollo Leoniceno, on the origin of syphilis to refute his colleague on the Leipzig medical faculty, Simon Pistoris. Jerome Schurff, the jurist and humanist, was recruited for Wittenberg from Tübingen by Staupitz. Hermann von der Bussche was called as the first professor of rhetoric. Nickolaus Marschalk was chosen to teach Greek and probably also Hebrew. Von der Bussche left Wittenberg in 1503 and Marschalk in 1505. Christoph Scheurl was enlisted for the

scholars among his closest friends and acquaintances. He was, however, no humanist himself[21] and possessed few of the linguistic tools for biblical study. Apart from German, he was proficient only in Latin. Though he betrayed a typically medieval interest in the history and derivation of words, he could not be called a philologist. He shared with the humanists a passion for returning to the sources (though his admiration for their learning did not stir him to master Greek and Hebrew himself), a respect for the Fathers as the most profound and sympathetic interpreters of Sacred Scripture, and a permanent distaste for hairsplitting and partisan theological debates.

The sermons on Job utilize the standard conventions of medieval homiletical theory.[22] Unlike Gregory the Great, whose *Moralia* on the book of Job form the background and inspiration for Staupitz's own sermons, Staupitz does not follow the Patristic practice of free, verse-by-verse commentary on the text. Instead he imposes an external outline on each sermon: three major points (in form always the same) with three subpoints marshalled under each of them. The text chosen for the day is brief, perhaps only a fragment of a verse, sometimes merely a single word. The motto for all thirty-four sermons, which Staupitz uses as a superscription over each homily, is the famous saying of Job as he hears the first reports

---

faculty of Wittenberg in 1506 and composed the new statutes for the University of Wittenberg in 1508, using a thoroughly humanistic rhetorical style. The humanists added to their ranks the Italian scholar Ricardus Sbrulius and the poet Georg Sibutus. Tilemann Conradi, who was a student at Wittenberg and a member of the humanist circle around Sbrulius, became a teacher of Greek in the faculty of arts in 1511. In 1507 Jodocus Trutfetter began to represent the *via moderna* at Wittenberg. Trutfetter was a scholastic theologian with an understanding of and a sympathy for the humanist movement. Staupitz knew these humanists and saw to it that humanism was given a place in the university.

21. Junghans observes, "Einfluß des Humanismus," p. 88: "Von Staupitz ist zwar selbst literarisch nicht als Humanist hervorgetreten, aber es läßt sich auch nicht-übersehen, daß er mindestens seit 1497 mit dem Humanismus in Berührung kam und mit Humanisten befreundet war. Sowohl der Augustinereremitenorden als auch die Wittenberger Universität verdanken ihm, daß er beide nicht nur nicht zu antihumanistischen Streit anführte, sondern in beiden Körperschaften die Humanisten gewähren ließ, ja sie sogar förderte."

22. On medieval homiletical theory see Ray C. Petry, *No Uncertain Sound* (Philadelphia: Westminster Press, 1948), pp. 1–44; Th.-M. Charland, O.P., *Artes Praedicandi, Contribution à l'histoire de la rhétorique au moyen âge* (Ottawa and Paris, 1936); Anton Linsenmayer, *Geschichte der Predigt in Deutschland* (Munich, 1886); Harry Caplan, "Rhetorical Invention in Some Medieval Tractates on Preaching," *Speculum* 2 (1927): 284–95; "The Four Senses of Scriptural Interpretation and the Medieval Theory of Preaching," *Speculum* 4 (1929), 282–90; "Classical Rhetoric and the Medieval Theory of Preaching," *Classical Philology* 28 (1933): 73–96. Cf. Petry, *No Uncertain Sound*, pp. 311–25, for further bibliographical suggestions.

of the totally unexpected disasters which have struck him down: "The Lord
gave and the Lord has taken away; blessed be the name of the Lord."

The repetition of this motto is more than pious convention. No conviction is more fundamental to Staupitz than his belief that at the center of
the book of Job and of the Old Testament—and, indeed, of Christian theology generally—one finds the praise and adoration of God.[23] God is to
be praised and loved for his own sake and not for the sake of his benefits.
Therefore God can and must be praised in the destitution and utter deso-
lation of Job's situation. Christian theology always begins with the praise
of God and not with the vulnerability, real or merely potential, of the human situation. As the theologian begins with the praise of God, so must
the preacher and interpreter of the biblical text. *Dominus dedit etc.*

The text of the day is cited, followed almost immediately by a quotation
from Gregory's *Moralia*. The citation of an authority in the introduction
to a sermon is not unusual in medieval preaching, though it is certainly
not required. The introduction is frequently brief. Still it may, as in sermon six, be fairly lengthy and can, indeed, call on other authorities in
addition to or in the place of Gregory. The introduction to sermon six, to
keep to the same example, appeals to Thomas Aquinas, Augustine, and
Paul, omitting altogether the customary citation from the *Moralia*.[24]

Each text of Job is then divided into three principal parts. Following
the suggestion of Gregory the Great, who remarks that Scripture is a
mirror of life, Job and his experiences are first portrayed as a reflection
of the human situation (*speculi vivendi propositivus*);[25] the image of Job
is then impressed on the members of the congregation gathered to hear
the sermon (*receptae imaginis considerativus*);[26] and, finally, the practical
implications of the text are driven home by the preacher as the congregation is charged with the responsibility of exercising the virtues clarified
in the mirror of Scripture (*virtutis acquisitae reservativus*).[27] The division
seems awkward and Staupitz has some difficulty making it work.

23. *Hiob* 30.229.2–4. Cf. *Hiob* 5.32.26–33; 8.56.14–22. In the *Libellus* 3 Staupitz
repeats this view: "Finis itaque creationis et reparationis est laus creatoris redemp-
torisque."

24. *Hiob* 6.33.7–35.21.   26. *Hiob* Introductio.2.11.
25. *Hiob* Introductio.2.9–10.

27. *Hiob* Introductio.2.13. Frequently in medieval sermons the theme parts were
rhymed. The rhymes served as an aid to the memory and, indeed, dictionaries of
rhymed sermon parts were available for the medieval preacher who could not make
a rhyme of his own. The repetition of the *tivus* ending of the sermon parts, though
not a perfect rhyme, is clearly a mnemonic device, calculated to jog the memory of the
preacher and to assist the congregation to retain more easily what they have heard.

The first point, the *speculi vivendi propositivus,* is itself further divided into three subpoints, corresponding roughly to the major divisions of the text as a whole. The first subpoint describes how the glory of God is revealed by the text. The second and third suggest a virtue one might aspire to emulate and outline the best way for achieving it.[28] Threefold divisions are also suggested for the other major points, but Staupitz rarely has time to develop them—which, considering the inorganic nature of this structure, may have all been for the best.

On the whole, one could say that Staupitz uses in a relaxed and less sharply defined way the threefold exegetical scheme of Gregory the Great, who patiently and painstakingly distinguished the historical sense of the text from the allegorical and moral before explaining the meaning of Job in all three senses.[29] One searches in vain in these sermons for a reference to the Quadriga or for the late medieval distinction between the historical-literal and the historical-prophetic meaning of the Old Testament. Staupitz has no interest in the anagogical meaning of the text (few late medieval preachers would have had much curiosity about it in any case). Nor does the young Staupitz proceed like the old, or at least middle-aged, Staupitz from a Christological center in his exegesis. Even the ordinary gloss on Job is more explicitly Christological than are these sermons. Apart from his elaborate homiletical structure, Staupitz is casual about relating his approach to Scripture to traditional hermeneutical methods. He interprets the allegorical and moral sense of the text, but rarely labels in advance what he is doing.

While Staupitz praises Gregory rather fulsomely and quotes his commentary on Job in almost every sermon, his indebtedness to Gregory is less profound than appearances might lead one to believe. At times, of course, the indebtedness is real enough, as the second major section of Staupitz's first sermon makes abundantly clear.[30] Nevertheless, Staupitz introduces a great many subjects not treated by Gregory in his commentary and develops the themes which he does borrow with considerable freedom. Nowhere, for example, in the first three books of the *Moralia* will one find as rich a treatment of predestination as one can discover in the eleventh sermon of Staupitz.[31] Gregory's remarks on this text (Job 1:6) stimulate Staupitz to inquire about the nature and extent of angelic

---

28. *Hiob* Introductio.2.14–21.

29. Gregory the Great, *Moralia in Iob* 3.118. References are to the edition *Morales sur Job,* Sources chrétiennes 32 (Paris, 1950).

30. *Hiob* 1.2.27–4.13.   31. *Hiob* 11.91.27–95.19.

knowledge in relation to the knowledge of God and man.[32] But the question is answered for Staupitz by apt quotations from Augustine and Giles rather than from Gregory.[33]

Gregory uses two hermeneutical devices, which he derives from St. Augustine.[34] Staupitz also uses them,[35] though it is impossible to say whether he learns them directly from Augustine or indirectly from Gregory and the medieval exegetical tradition. The first device is the rule of Tychonius expounded by Augustine in *De doctrina Christiana* III.xxxi.44: "Of the Lord and His Body." Under this rule what is predicated of Christ the head of the Church may also be predicated of the Church itself and, to some extent, though the rule is not absolutely reversible, what is predicated of the body may also be attributed to the head. Furthermore, under the rule of genus and species (III.xxxiv.47) what is true of the part, the Christian or faithful soul, may also be affirmed concerning the whole; viz., the Church of which that soul is a constituent part. Staupitz makes, on the whole, prudent use of these hermeneutical rules and does not sprinkle his exegesis with questionable analogies.

But while Staupitz employs these traditional hermeneutical devices with commendable caution, his sermons are not free of some of the worst faults of the late medieval preacher. He ruthlessly atomizes the text he has chosen by focusing on a word or phrase and allowing a fragment of the text to serve as a motto for an essay which, speaking charitably, is only tangentially related to the passage under discussion. For example, Staupitz uses the text, "And there were born to him seven sons and three daughters," as an occasion for preaching on the nature of Christian marriage[36]— a worthy subject, no doubt, but hardly a concern uppermost in the mind of the author of Job. Even more unforgivable is Staupitz's unfortunate, though happily infrequent, inclination to make a text crawl on all fours by emphasizing each successive word in turn.[37]

32. *Hiob* 11.84.24ff.   33. *Hiob* 11.86.31ff.
34. For "Of the Lord and His Body," see Gregory, *Moralia*, Praefatio VI.14.136–137. "Genus and Species" is illustrated by the remark "quod in Johannis Apocalypsi per septem Ecclesiarum numerum universalis Ecclesia designatur." *Moralia*, Praefatio VIII.18.139. The two hermeneutical principles may be summarized as the *caput-corpus-membra* schema.
35. *Hiob* 30.234.27–29; 31.241.24–35; 32.243.25ff.
36. *Hiob* 6.33.7–44.21.
37. *Hiob* 14.127.22–25. In this sermon Staupitz divides the text, "Numquid consi-derasti servum meum Job?," into (a) "Numquid considerasti meum?," which demonstrates the honor of God; (b) "Numquid considerasti servum meum?," which shows

These unsatisfactory homiletical habits are later abandoned for a hermeneutical method which more faithfully reflects the exegetical content of the text. This shift is already apparent in the German sermons of 1512–15 and has crystallized in the *Libellus* of 1517. Staupitz's constant immersion in Scripture and in the practice of exegesis slowly reshapes his hermeneutic. The later Staupitz no longer imposes rigid outlines on the text, but rather allows the logic of Scripture to mold the structure of his sermons. While he still makes use of the medieval rhetorical and exegetical tradition, he subordinates that tradition to the biblical vision of the unfolding drama of redemption.

Unfortunately, the sermons on Job do not address directly the question of the relationship of the two testaments or the distinction between letter and spirit. Staupitz's systematic reflections on those thorny issues are contained in the German writings and sermons of 1518–23,[38] well after Luther had forged his own new hermeneutic. They cannot therefore be used as the basis for comparison with Luther's developing position in 1513–15.

Some things, however, are clear, even in the early sermons on Job. The Old Testament is inspired and exists for the edification of the Church.[39] There is nothing in it without at least some value for the Christian congregation in the present. Like the New Testament, the book of Job witnesses to Jesus Christ, whom Job knew by direct revelation.[40] Despite the fact that Job was a Gentile, not a Christian, and lived outside the Church and its sacraments, he was redeemed and perfected by the grace of God in Jesus Christ.[41] The Old Testament and the New reach into each other, though the Christian interpreter must stand in the New if he wishes to comprehend what the book of Job means and implies at every level of its significance.

Staupitz's exegetical approach to the Old Testament can be demonstrated by an appeal to almost any of his sermons.[42] We shall limit our

---

the image of virtue; and (c) "Numquid considerasti servum meum Job?," which edifies the neighbor. For a similar treatment of the text, "Numquid frustra Job timet dominum?," see 15.131.35–38.

38. For a treatment of these later observations on the relation of letter and spirit, see my *Misericordia Dei*, pp. 171–81.

39. *Hiob* 1.2.27–35.

40. *Hiob* 11.98.32–35.

41. *Hiob* 1.2.41–3.24.

42. For a useful discussion of the historical circumstances which prompted Staupitz to preach on Job, see the introduction to the 1927 edition of the sermons on Job by

observations to four:[43] sermon one,[44] which sets the tone for the sermons which are to follow; sermon two,[45] which analyzes the virtue of simplicity (particularly against the vice of curiosity);[46] sermon six,[47] which characterizes the state of matrimony and sketches in the elements of a sexual ethic;[48] and sermon eleven,[49] which places human temptation in the context of providence and predestination.

If one examines the form of these sermons, one cannot fail to be struck, first of all, by the strict application in them of the standard medieval homiletical method: three main points (invariably the same in structure) with three subpoints faithfully ranged under each heading. Indeed, Staupitz's insistence on the repetition in each sermon of the same three major

---

Ernst Wolf, *Staupitz Tübinger Predigten*, QFRG 8 (Leipzig, 1927), pp. vii–xiv. Wolf reads Hiob 1.6 as *ex iniuncto*, which makes good sense when seen against 1.20 and 1.27.

43. It is not clear how many of the thirty-four sermons actually were preached or whether the form in which they were preached differs in any significant way from the form in which they were written. Sermon six, for example, ends with the words (6.44.21): "Sed hoc legentibus relinquendum est." This seems to imply an audience of readers rather than a congregation of auditors, an impression confirmed by Staupitz's earlier remark in the same sermon (6.44.11): "Non expedit ad punctum scribere quae sencio." Again in 10.83.24 and 25.199.39 Staupitz refers to readers and can even allude to himself as a writer rather than as a preacher (12.105.17). Ernst Wolf is of the opinion that the thirty-four sermons which have survived represent Staupitz's own later report and reworking of sermons which he had already delivered. Cf. Ernst Wolf, *Staupitz und Luther*, QFRG 9 (Leipzig, 1927), pp. 16–18. If this surmise is true, the written sermons may excise material actually used in preaching, perhaps more popular in nature, and replace it with technical material chiefly of interest to other friars. For reasons such as this Wolf was forced to the conclusion: "Die 34 Predigten selbst werden zum Urteil über Staupitz als Prediger nicht viel beitragen können, denn es handelt sich zwar z.T. um Sermone, die vermutlich vorgetragen wurden, aber ihre Niederschrift erfolgte dann wohl nachträglich." *Staupitz und Luther*, p. 16.

44. The text of this sermon is found in *Hiob* 1.2.27–1.6.27. While there probably is a difference between the sermons as preached and as written, one ought to be wary of exaggerating that difference. The later treatises of Staupitz reflect both in form and content the character of his popular preaching. While it is possible that the written sermons on Job represent a complex elaboration of much simpler homilies, one must explain why Staupitz no longer felt obligated to dress up the substance of his popular German sermons in the same way.

45. The text of this sermon is found in *Hiob* 2.6.29–2.11.35.

46. For an interesting treatment of the subject of *curiositas* in the late Middle Ages and Reformation, see H. A. Oberman, *Contra vanam curiositatem*, Theologische Studien 113 (Zurich, 1974).

47. For the text of this sermon see *Hiob* 6.33.7–6.44.21.

48. Sermon six on marriage may, indeed, be directed toward a lay audience, though the average congregation would make heavy weather of the learned quotations with which this sermon is peppered. Wolf does not believe that this sermon was ever preached. *Staupitz und Luther*, p. 16.

49. The text of this sermon is reproduced in *Hiob* 11.83.27–11.100.22.

divisions—the mirror of life,[50] the impression of the image on the viewer,[51] and the exercise of the acquired virtue[52]—together with the inflexible sub-

50. The identical structure is used in each sermon. Perhaps this can best be illustrated by outlining the structure in general and ranging the specific points made by each sermon below. In what follows S.1, S.2, and S.6 designate sermons 1, 2, and 6 in *Hiob*.

I. The mirror of life
    A. The manifestation of the glory of God
        S.1 Job is an example of the mercy of God.
        S.2 Job is *simplex*, i.e., *sine plica*, free from the crease of curiosity.
        S.6 The text presents three images:
            a. The power of God by which he created male and female
            b. The wisdom of God by which he orders all things sweetly
            c. The goodness of God which restores a damaged human race.
    B. The image of virtue
        S.1 Job is a lily among thorns; evil makes his goodness all the more desirable.
        S.2 Job is *simplex*, free from falsity and deceit.
        S.6 The sexual act in marriage is:
            a. Not bad (against heretics who affirm the opposite)
            b. Good, because God commanded it
            c. Meritorious, when informed by love.
    C. The edification of the neighbor
        S.1 We find company in our misery in the saintly pattern of the life of Job.
        S.2 Job is *simplex*, free from cunning and trickery.
        S.6 Marriage has three goods:
            a. Fidelity
            b. Children
            c. Sacrament; permanent and indissoluble relationship.

51. The identical structure is employed by Staupitz in making his second major point and can be illustrated in the same way.

II. The impression of the image on the viewer
    A. First principle
        S.1 Sorrowful reflection over things past
        S.2 Uniformity of morals and customs; important for members of religious orders
        S.6 Strength and constancy of reason
    B. Second principle
        S.1 Careful foresight of things future
        S.2 Contemplation of the eternal; for contemplatives
        S.6 Difference from animals
    C. Third principle
        S.1 Precise knowledge of things present
        S.2 Example of the saints; for secular clergy and laity
        S.6 Mental delight

52. The third point continues much the same structure.

III. The exercise of the acquired virtue
    A. First effect
        S.1 *Intellectus*; we cannot love what we do not know.
        S.2 Uniformity involves the recognition that not all have the same gifts.
        S.6 The ordered consideration of circumstances

division of the first article into (a) the manifestation of the glory of God,[53] (b) the image of virtue,[54] and (c) the edification of the neighbor,[55] constitutes, even by late medieval standards, something of a tour de force.

  B. Second effect
     S.1 *Affectus;* sorrow only possible for those who realize that the goods of eternity could be lost.
     S.2 Contemplatives must realize that they are saved by grace and not by spiritual discipline.
     S.6 Human disposition of the member in the act.
  C. Third effect
     S.1 *Actus;* foresight leads to careful action in the present.
     S.2 Experiences of some saints more helpful to some Christians than to others.
     S.6 The worthy celebration of a stated time.

53. In sermon 11 Staupitz develops the first subpoint in this way:
I. The mirror of life
  A. The manifestation of the glory of God. The glory is revealed in divine omniscience.
     1. Divine knowledge knows everything.
     2. Divine knowledge causes things. This point is supported by quotations from Giles of Rome, I *Sent.* d. 38 q.1, Aristotle's *Metaphysics*, and Augustine, *De Trinitate* 15.13.
     3. Divine knowledge preordains determined ends for all things. This point is supported by Thomas Aquinas, II *Summa contra Gentiles* c.23.

54. In sermon 11 the second subpoint under the first article is developed as follows:
I. The mirror of life.
  B. The image of virtue. Divine providence gives man the courage to sustain the temptations ordained for him. See especially Giles of Rome, I *Sent.* d.39 q.4. One can list some definitions of providence:
        a. Governance. Cf. Augustine.
        b. Care. Cf. John of Damascus.
        c. Disposition. Cf. Augustine.
     1. Various states of salvation: monasticism, marriage, virginity, priesthood, etc. One who faces temptation should ask whether he is in a state in which it is possible to be saved. Cf. Bonaventure, III *Sent.* d.30. God ordains duties for each state.
     2. God provides the power for each state.
     3. Power must be joined to action to be effective.

55. The third subpoint of the first article of sermon 11 is explained by Staupitz in this way:
I. The mirror of life
  C. The edification of the neighbor. The neighbor is edified by a contemplation of predestination.
     1. The truest sign of predestination is conformity to Christ in bearing the cross of undeserved suffering.
     2. The elect are called through grace and there is no calling without temptation.
     3. The called are justified through the sacraments of the Church, especially through penance. Augustine, *Enarratio in Ps. 55*, is important for Staupitz in the development of this point.

The introduction to each sermon is shorter than the usual *exordium* and cannot be regarded as complete in itself.[56] But apart from this slight variation from recommended practice, the sermons conform, at least in their basic structural design, to the homiletical models advocated by late medieval handbooks on the *ars praedicandi*. In fact, one might reasonably infer, both from the theological content of the sermons and their carefully constructed form, that Staupitz regarded his sermons as examples of good homiletical practice which the younger friars in the Augustinian *Stift* would do well to emulate.[57] Never again in any of the German sermons which have survived does Staupitz adhere so single-mindedly to the requirements of the homiletical textbooks.

The sermons make only limited use of commentaries and the medieval exegetical tradition.[58] To be sure, Staupitz does cite Gregory the Great, *Moralia in Iob*, and Augustine, *Enarrationes in Psalmos*, with great regularity, but that is probably as much for the general theological content of these writings as for any specific exegetical help they might offer in interpreting the text of Job. When Staupitz explains the meaning of the name "Job," always a favorite occupation of medieval preachers who are fascinated with the etymologies of words, he agrees with the *Glossa ordinaria*[59] and repeats the opinion of Gregory that Job means "dolens,"[60] an educated

56. The introduction to sermon six is more nearly complete in itself than the introductions to the other three sermons. It poses the question, What is true felicity? which it answers with the help of the *Nicomachean Ethics* of Aristotle and apt quotations from Thomas Aquinas and Augustine.

57. I think it probable that Staupitz applies the label *ad vulgum* to the sermons as written and not just to the sermons as preached. While there may, indeed, be a difference between the sermons as delivered in the Augustinian *Stift* and the later manuscript, Staupitz's understanding of *neque scolastice disputando sed ad vulgum praedicando* is broad enough to include the written sermons with all their learned citations of philosophical and theological literature. Johannes Altenstaig reports that he heard Staupitz preach "non solum coram populo sed etiam coram summis viris et doctissimis," when he was a student in Tübingen. I do not think, however, that *ad vulgum* is a synonym in Staupitz's mind for *coram populo*. On Altenstaig see Wolf, *Staupitz und Luther*, p. 16.

58. This is in sharp contrast to Martin Luther, who consults a wide range of commentaries on the Psalms as he prepares his lectures on them. In this connection see Gerhard Ebeling, "Luthers Auslegung des 14.(15.) Psalms in der ersten Psalmenvorlesung im Vergleich mit der exegetischen Tradition," *Lutherstudien* I (Tübingen, 1971), p. 132, footnote 1. Luther specifically cites Augustine, Cassiodorus, *Glossa ordinaria, Glossa interlinearis*, Peter Lombard, Hugo de S. Caro Card., Nicolaus of Lyra, Paul of Burgos, Matthias Doering, John of Turrecremata, Faber Stapulensis, and what Luther believes to be a work of Jerome.

59. For the ordinary gloss see Walafrid Strabo, *Glossa ordinaria, Liber Job, PL* 113, col. 750.

60. Gregory, *Moralia*, I.xi.15.149: "Job namque, ut diximus, interpretatus dolens: Hus vero consiliator." Cf. *Hiob* 1.4.24–25.

guess which owes more to a knowledge of the plot of the story than to any exact acquaintance with the Hebrew language. Staupitz gives the impression that he approaches the book of Job as a dogmatic theologian rather than as a biblical scholar in the narrower sense of the term.[61] Certainly he interprets Job with the aid of theological treatises written on subjects suggested to him by the text rather than with the aid of lexicons, grammars, and commentaries—the kind of tools one would expect to find on the desk of a humanist scholar.

Staupitz's appeal to theological essays and dogmatic treatises rather than to biblical commentaries and grammars is not altogether surprising when one considers the usual structure of the medieval university sermon[62] and the leisurely pace at which Staupitz strolls through the book of Job. He preaches no less than five sermons on Job 1:1, two on 1:3, and two on 1:7. Obviously no commentaries can hope to provide enough grist for a mill which turns with such monumental deliberation. Quotations from theological authorities buttress his exegetical points just as illustrations from life or pious tales from the ever-present collections of exempla might support the far simpler homily of a village parson.

Of the nine methods for expanding a sermon recommended by the anonymous author of the *Tractatulus solemnis de arte et vero modo praedicandi*,[63] Staupitz makes use in these four sermons of seven. His favorite method is the concordance of authorities. While he tells no anecdotes and makes few contemporary allusions,[64] he reads to his congregation of friars extensive passages from a wide variety of authorities: philosophical, theological, and exegetical. He discusses words, such as *simplex*;[65] multiplies senses,[66] though he shows more interest in the allegorical and

61. Ernst Wolf observed, *Staupitz und Luther*, p. 21: "Was die Art der Predigten anlangt, so zeigt die Übersicht der Themen und Texte bereits, daß für Staupitz der Sermon offenbar die geeignete Form zur Entwicklung seiner theologischen Ansichten bildet. Erbauliche Rede, Auslegung der Schrift and Behandlung dogmatischer Fragen finden hier Platz; die letztere ist beherrschend."

62. Cf. Petry, *No Uncertain Sound*, p. 10.

63. The nine methods are: (1) concordance of authorities, (2) discussion of words, (3) explanations of the properties of things, (4) multiplication of senses, (5) analogies and natural truths, (6) marking of an opposite, (7) comparisons, (8) interpretation of a name, and (9) multiplication of synonyms. Cf. Harry Caplan, "The Four Senses of Scriptural Interpretation and the Medieval Theory of Preaching," *Speculum* 4 (1929): 282. In these four sermons Staupitz does not explain the properties of things or multiply synonyms.

64. He does, however, allude briefly to the Turks in 8.61.19ff. and provide an illustration from Roman history in 8.61.14ff.

65. *Hiob* 2.6.29ff.

66. Observe as well what Staupitz says in *Hiob* 19.155.12ff.

tropological sense of Scripture than in its literal or anagogical meaning; and interprets names, of which "Job" is the outstanding example.[67] He can draw analogies[68] and appeal to natural truths ("Misery loves company,"[69] "Nature abhors inaction,"[70] or "Motion is from a contrary to a contrary").[71] Furthermore, his discussion of Satan and the angels allows him an opportunity to mark opposites[72] and make comparisons.[73] Not only in the general structure of his sermon, but even in the development of his argument, Staupitz follows closely the recommended models of medieval preaching.

One should not underestimate the extent to which Staupitz uses Scripture as a commentary on Scripture. His biblical citations are widely scattered, though the Psalms and the Pauline corpus seem to predominate. There is an interesting interplay in sermon 11 between Romans 8, Psalm 55, and the exegetical comments of St. Augustine.[74] When Staupitz returns to the theme of predestination in his sermons at Nuremberg, he moves from Psalm 84 to Romans 8 to a critique of certain interpreters of St. Augustine.[75] Paul does not, however, serve as the basis for any criticism of St. Augustine either in the *Libellus* or in the sermons on Paul.

Augustine, finally, provides the spectacles through which Staupitz reads Job, Paul, the Psalms, indeed the whole of Scripture. While Staupitz quotes Thomas Aquinas and a host of scholastic authorities, their comments appear subordinate to Scripture understood from a strongly Augustinian point of view. On the other hand, Scripture never becomes the basis from which Staupitz takes his later authorities to task. The sermons are not polemical; they are not even mildly critical of the sources he uses. Staupitz does not carry an Abelardian *sic et non* mentality with him into the pulpit.

---

67. *Hiob* 1.4.24–25.
68. Note the natural analogy between the normal day and eternity and between the sun and the divine light of knowledge, providence, and predestination in *Hiob* 11.84.24ff.
69. *Hiob* 1.4.2–3.   71. *Hiob* 1.5.17–18.
70. *Hiob* 11.91.15–16; 13.124.17.   72. *Hiob* 11.99.28–34.
73. *Hiob* 11.86.31ff. is filled with comparisons between divine, human, and angelic knowledge.
74. *Hiob* 11.91.27–11.95.19.
75. *Libellus* 6–28. Cf. especially 28: "Consequens est dictum illud vulgare quod Augustino nostro ascribunt in sensu quem minime defendi posse: 'Si non es predestinatus, fac predestineris.'" For an important discussion of this question, see the stimulating essay by H. A. Oberman, "'Tuus sum, salvum me fac,' Augustinréveil zwischen Renaissance und Reformation," in *Scientia Augustiniana: Studien über Augustinus, den Augustinismus und den Augustinerorden*, ed. C. P. Mayer and W. Eckermann (Würzburg, 1975), pp. 349–94.

The book of Job provides Staupitz with an occasion for writing a series of doctrinal tracts. The power of these tracts derives from the ideas they propose and the authorities they cite. In form they are unremarkable. Staupitz intended them to be *ad vulgum* in the sense that any university sermon is, one would hope, less technical in its argument and more practical in its intention than a lecture on the agent intellect. But the sermons are not popular in the sense that they are addressed to a simple and uneducated congregation.

Job is the framework on which Staupitz hangs the central themes of Christian dogmatic and moral theology. It is popular theology in the sense that it is not "contentious" (*rixosa*). It uses the story of Scripture, familiar to all, as the structure which suggests and determines the unfolding succession of theological topics. This impulse to make theology biblical rather than systematic is still rigidly confined by the strict homiletical framework to which Staupitz has committed himself. When that artificial framework dissolves, as it does in the *Libellus* of 1517, Staupitz writes a theology which is both biblical and systematic, systematic precisely because it reflects the logic of the unfolding story of God's saving acts in history.

II. *Luther as an Interpreter of the Psalms*

Luther's lectures on the Psalms (1513–15)[76] are much more extensive than Staupitz's sermons on Job (1497–98). It is therefore not surprising that Luther has far more to say about the nature of Holy Scripture and the proper methods for interpreting it than does Staupitz. Furthermore, unlike Staupitz, who is innocent of Hebrew and who makes little use of the medieval exegetical tradition beyond Augustine and Gregory the Great, Luther attempts to grapple with the original text of the Psalms and utilizes the full range of medieval and humanist exegetical tools in his quest for the deeper meaning of Scripture. As a result Luther's theological reflections grow much more organically out of the text than do Staupitz's, though neither theologian has any idea of aspiring to be a historian of the life and thought of Israel in the manner of a modern phenomenologist of religion.

76. Ebeling is quite correct when he points toward the astonishing "Einheitlichkeit des Impulses und der Thematik" in the *Dictata super Psalterium*. Gerhard Ebeling, *Lutherstudien I* (Tübingen, 1971), p. 11. It is all the more astonishing when one considers that the *Dictata* is not a systematic treatise but a commentary on 150 psalms.

What is particularly remarkable about Luther's early hermeneutical theory is the extent to which he uses metaphors drawn from eucharistic theology. The ancient Fathers had observed—one thinks in this connection of the Cappadocians—that whereas ordinary food is changed by natural processes into a human body, the sacred food of the eucharist reverses the usual metabolic process and changes the mortal body of the Christian into the immortal food which it eats. This sacramental language is applied by Luther without further ado to the study of Scripture. The power of Scripture is so great that it transforms those who study it into itself, the lover into the thing loved.[77]

Like the sacraments Scripture is a gift of God to the Church, a gift which never resides simply in the Church's power.[78] The prophets never stand at our beck and call and are not obliged to render up their secrets to the first doctor of divinity who schedules a series of university lectures on them. Luther has no intention of denigrating the role of theological learning, but learning has its limits. Scripture imposes its own meaning.[79] It is the Bible and not our learned exegesis which binds the soul to God.[80]

Exegesis is not merely an intellectual activity at which innate cleverness gives one an advantage over the slower-witted (though it is that, too). To interpret the Bible and interpret it correctly one must meet certain conditions which the text imposes on its interpreters. These preconditions are moral and spiritual as well as intellectual. What Luther has particularly in mind is humility.[81] Humility opens the mind to God just as pride dulls the sharpest intellect and keeps it from the truth.[82]

From what Luther has said so far, it is not surprising that he regards the interpretation of Scripture as a public event which takes place within the sphere of the Church. The Church, says Luther in language as uncompromising as any Cyprian ever used, is the gate of salvation[83] and there is no true knowledge of God outside it.[84] The Church's rule of faith is a hermeneutical landmark which delimits the area within which the exegesis of Scripture may be pursued. We ought not to reject out of hand any interpretation of the Bible which conforms to the rule of faith, however much

---

77. *WA* 3.397.7–12.   78. *WA* 3.516.40–517.4.
79. *WA* 4.318.3–6. This is a fairly sharp warning against eisegesis and a reminder that the true sense of Scripture is the *sensus nobis extraneus* which we ought humbly to receive.
80. *WA* 4.436.21–23.   82. *WA* 3.517.22–25.
81. *WA* 3.515.15–18.   83. *WA* 4.25.12–17.
84. *WA* 3.268.37–38: "Extra enim Ecclesiam non est cognitio vera Dei."

we may prefer another interpretation to it.[85] There is, after all, the possibility that our interpretation may need correction, even if that correction comes from a quarter which we regard as unwelcome. Sometimes a dull friar or an unlettered layman or an autocratic bishop may perceive a truth to which we have been insensitive. The student of Scripture is a member of a community to which he is responsible and from which he receives correction and encouragement.

Since the interpretation of Scripture is a public event, the magisterium of the Church has an important role to play in it. God wishes for men to be saved through the agency of other men.[86] The Pauline image of the body in which each member has something to contribute toward the common good seems to be the controlling metaphor for Luther. True humility keeps everything in perspective. No interpreter of the Bible, however brilliant, can afford to rely solely on his own intellectual gifts.[87] Pride leads inevitably to heresy, the exaltation of one's private judgment over the authentic sense of Scripture.[88]

Luther demonstrates a high regard for the office of doctor in the Church,[89] not merely the doctors of the ancient Church[90] but the preachers and teachers of his own time as well.[91] The doctor or preacher is a tongue of the Church.[92] By his teaching or preaching he generates sons of Christ in the womb of the gospel.[93] There are, of course, doctors who are teachers by human authorization alone and whose teaching never penetrates the

85. *WA* 3.517.33–40. Luther gives a personal example of this in *WA* 3.518.2ff.

86. Luther speaks of the *magisterium hominis discreti*, by which he may have in mind the *doctores et praedicatores*, and the *magisterium superioris*, by which he may have in mind the *episcopi vel praelati*. *WA* 4.211.15–19. Luther has already made it clear in his earlier writings that he is willing to submit his judgment in a disputed question to the magisterium of the Church. *BoA* 5.7.6 (cf. the uncorrected reading in *WA* 9.43.7). Jared Wicks in his review of Scott Hendrix's *Ecclesia in Via* also calls attention to the young Luther's concern with obedience to the hierarchy: "On Ps. 121.5 in the last extended scholion of the lectures, Luther treats the respective roles of superior and subject in the Church. Surprisingly, he portrays Christian righteousness as consisting precisely in obedience to ecclesiastical superiors: 'iustitia pertinet ad inferiorem . . . , quia est humilitas, obedientia, et resignata subiectio propriae voluntatis superiori' (*WA* 4, 405)." *Theological Studies* 36 (1975): 186.

87. *WA* 4.83.11–15.

88. *WA* 3.444.1–10.

89. *WA* 3.170.12–20. Luther is not solely concerned with the office of doctor in the Church, which he interprets much more broadly than just the office of university professor. Friars who preach are just as much *doctores* as the professor of Holy Scripture at Wittenberg. On the offices in the Church see Joseph Vercruysse, *Fidelis Populus* (Wiesbaden, 1968), pp. 165–86.

90. *WA* 4.318.1–2.

91. *WA* 3.139.20–24.

92. *WA* 3.295.27–30.

93. *WA* 3.454.30–33.

hearts of their listeners.[94] But where true doctors preach the Word of God, there the Church is created and nourished.[95] In fact, it is the perseverance of the preached Word of Christ which guarantees for Luther the perseverance of faith in the Church.[96] The indefectibility of the Church is grounded in this proclamation of the truth, hidden from sight[97] but accessible to the ear which hears and trusts it.[98]

While Luther exalts the office of doctor, he also has biting words of criticism for certain contemporary theologians who never grow tired of arguing over sacred mysteries and whose certitude seems to grow in inverse proportion to the likelihood of finding a solution to any of their disputes.[99] The highest theology is not the cacophony of the scholastic doctors, but the awesome silences of negative theology.[100] At the same time, while Luther rebukes what he regards as vain curiosity,[101] he also opposes the illusions of the mystics and religious enthusiasts who wish to dwell nakedly in God.[102] That is, of course, impossible. The New Testament asserts with inescapable clarity that the pilgrim who trudges toward the heavenly Jerusalem lives by faith and not by sight.

The fact that the interpreter of the Bible has a public responsibility and submits his exegesis for public scrutiny does not mean, of course, that his research and meditation on the meaning of Scripture is not an intensely private affair. Luther cannot recommend private meditation highly enough. He calls it *cogitatio in medio cordis*[103] and swears that it is the *summa, efficacissima et brevissima eruditio*.[104] Meditation, perhaps even meditation prolonged over many months, leads to those sudden and dramatic insights[105] which warm the heart and increase one's love for spiritual goods.[106] There is no biblical scholar worth his salt who does not meditate.

Luther employs three hermeneutical schemata, which he derives from the antecedent exegetical tradition, though he uses them in ways not wholly traditional: (1) the distinction of letter and spirit, (2) the Quadriga or fourfold meaning of Scripture—literal, allegorical, tropological, and anagogical, and (3) what one may call for lack of a better phrase the *caput-corpus-membra* schema.

94. *WA* 3.143.21–22.
95. *WA* 4.189.17–25.
96. *WA* 4.350.22–29.
97. *WA* 55².100.11–14.
98. *WA* 4.450.39ff.
99. *WA* 3.382.7–17.
100. *WA* 3.372.20–27.

101. *WA* 55².21.21–22.
102. *WA* 4.64.33–65.12.
103. *WA* 3.222.18–23.
104. *WA* 3.539.23–24.
105. *WA* 55².16.2–5.
106. *WA* 3.222.18–23.

1. *Letter and spirit.* The distinction of letter and spirit was traditionally understood in two principal ways: (a) as a means of distinguishing the deeper meaning of the biblical text (which edifies the Church) from the mere story told by the words (which from time to time does not) or (b) as a way of emphasizing the difference between the demands of God laid on the sinner without the gift of grace which would enable the sinner to meet them (i.e., the letter) and the gracious gifts of the Holy Spirit which enable otherwise helpless sinners to respond in a positive way to the law of God (i.e., the spirit). Luther has both meanings in mind as he utilizes the distinction, though he modifies the tradition somewhat to conform it to his own developing ideas of the central message of Scripture.

Letter as bare narrative has a positive role to play for Luther as for any medieval theologian. The historical meaning of the text is the basis of the allegorical, tropological, and anagogical senses and no theological position can be sustained which does not find expression somewhere in the letter of Scripture.[107] One cannot develop a dogmatic position on the basis of the allegorical, tropological, and anagogical senses alone. In that sense the letter is fundamental and unavoidable. Theology cannot circumvent the letter but must sink its pilings securely into it.

Far more frequently, however, Luther regards the letter negatively as a danger and temptation for the Church. To read the Old Testament as a collection of ancient stories concerning Near Eastern Semitic tribes and to miss the vital connection to Christ is to miss the deeper meaning of the text intended by the Holy Spirit.[108] The story outside Christ is death-dealing. Indeed, one might even say, in a paraphrase of Cyprian: *extra Christum nulla intelligentia,* outside Christ no understanding of the Bible.

The central message of Scripture is the message of the threefold work of God—in Christ,[109] in the Church,[110] and in us[111]—for the salvation of the world. This message is proclaimed in the Old Testament as well as the New. The prophets and saints of the Old Testament understood the message of the work of God spiritually and so received saving benefit from it.[112] The message took the form in the Old Testament of both law and promises. The law of Moses, however, can be understood according to the letter or according to the spirit, since the distinction of letter and spirit is primarily a distinction between two ways of relating to the same reality.

107. WA 55¹.4.20–21.
108. WA 55¹.2.9–11.
109. WA 3.369.2–10; 4.189.1–4.

110. WA 3.369.2–10; 4.189.1–4.
111. WA 3.541.38–542.2.
112. WA 55¹.92.16ff.

As letter the law of Moses provides a visible,[113] external righteousness valid before men but of no avail whatever before God.[114] The law of Moses is not bad in itself,[115] but only becomes a threat to human existence when it is read by scribes who lack the Spirit and who therefore mistake the shadow for the substance, the sign for the thing signified.[116]

The "thing" (res) signified by the law is the life, death, and resurrection of Jesus Christ.[117] This is the substance which casts its shadow back into the Old Testament.[118] It is invisible to the faithful synagogue, not because it is a heavenly archetype which transcends the world of sense data but because it is future. Like all future events, it cannot be seen.[119]

The prophecy of the Old Testament refers to Christ.[120] The promise of better things to come was preached to the Old Testament saints and heard by the ear of faith.[121] Even the law of Moses, spiritually understood, contains "words and signs of future works."[122] Therefore the Old Testament, which is the sign and contains the promises, cannot be correctly understood without the New, which is the thing signified, the fulfillment of the expectation of the prophets and of the law of Moses understood according to the spirit.[123] Indeed, the "spiritual law" (lex spiritualis) is the gospel.[124]

Just as the law of Moses may be grasped as sign and understood according to the spirit, so, too, the gospel may be understood according to the letter as law. The distinction between law and gospel is not a distinction between the Old and New Testaments any more than the possibility of responding according to the spirit or according to the letter is limited to one era in the history of salvation. Gospel and law belong to the history of Israel and to the life of the Church. Even the gospel is an impossible law without the inner aid of the Holy Spirit.[125] The law, as a message which

113. WA 3.455.29–33.
114. WA 3.116.5–8.
115. WA 4.306.8–19.
116. WA 3.318.24ff.
117. WA 3.318.18–24.
118. WA 55².67.16–19
119. WA 3.508.21–23.
120. WA 55¹.6.25ff.
121. WA 3.227.27–29.

122. WA 3.258.2–10. Ebeling observes that creation is also a sign which is fulfilled in Christ.

123. WA 55¹.6.26–27. Interestingly enough, when Luther speaks of Job as an example of one who is simplex, he does not have in mind Staupitz's exegesis of simplex as freedom from curiosity, deceit, and cunning, but the idea that Job keeps himself pure in fide futurorum. WA 4.251.31–34. Nothing could be more revealing of the difference in the approach of Luther and Staupitz to the tropological sense than this. For Staupitz the tropological sense is moral; for Luther it pertains to faith in the Word of Christ which is a testimony of future things. Cf. also WA 4.324.6–7.

124. WA 4.134.20: "Quia lex spiritualis et evangelium idem sunt." Cf. 55¹.92.16ff., especially the words: "Lex spiritualiter intellecta est idem cum evangelio."

125. WA 3.451.22–27.

is directed toward us (*ad nos*),[126] is powerless to free the inner man;[127] only the gospel as a word which penetrates us (*in nos*) is able to liberate the human personality from its bondage to egocentricity and its alienation from God.[128]

No wonder Luther exclaims that the ability to discern spirit from letter is what makes a theologian![129] Such an ability is not a natural human faculty but a gift of the Holy Spirit to the Church. What is at stake in the distinction of letter and spirit is a decision for or against God.[130] The distinction is not merely intellectual but implies and presupposes two different ways of conducting one's life: according to the spirit, i.e., in faith, humility, and obedience to God; or according to the letter, i.e., in unfaith, pride, and rebellion against God.

With this in mind, Luther defines what is meant by the spiritual understanding of Scripture. According to the philosophers, whose reflections on this matter are ultimately irrelevant for the interpreter of Scripture, *intellectus* is a human power. That is not, however, what is meant by *intellectus* when the subject under discussion is the meaning of Holy Scripture. In biblical language *intellectus* is defined by its object, in this case the "knowledge of the meaning of Christ" or simply the "wisdom of the cross of Christ."[131] What Luther has in view is not an abstract knowledge of Christ or assent to a series of propositions about him, but a faithful apprehension of the saving act of God in Christ as it is directed toward the Christian and his existence in the world. This kind of knowledge is not created by letters or by words but by the Holy Spirit.[132] It is trust in the revelation of God hidden under the form of a contrary appearance.

One of the most persistent themes in the *Dictata* is the motif of the hiddenness of God. Luther is concerned not simply with the hiddenness of God outside his revelation, important as that theme may be, but with the far more central problem of the hiddenness of God within his revelation. When God reveals himself, he simultaneously hides himself under the form of a contrary.[133]

The text which inspires Luther's reflections on the *absconditas sub contrario* is I Corinthians 1:18–31, where Paul celebrates the wisdom of

126. WA 4.9.28–29.

127. WA 55².7.1–6.

128. WA 3.456.11–17; 55².31.6ff.

129. WA 55¹.4.25–27.

130. Heinrich Bornkamm, *Luther and the Old Testament* (Philadelphia: Fortress Press, 1969), p. 88.

131. WA 3.176.3–10; 4.324.2–4.

132. WA 3.451.32–35.

133. WA 4.81.25–27; 55².106.16–19.

God in what the world regards as folly and the demonstration of the power of God in what men esteem as the decisive evidence of his weakness.[134] This theology of the cross implies that hiddenness is the form of God's revelation. The God who reveals himself in the pages of Holy Scripture is a God who works contrary to human expectation.[135] The work of God is therefore not visible to sight, since everything the eye sees provides impressive grounds for distrusting the promises of God. The eye sees weakness not strength, folly not wisdom, humiliation not victory. Consequently Luther pits the ear against the eye.[136] The Christian must hear by faith the promise which runs contrary to the empirical evidence his eye can assess and trust it.[137] Anyone who prefers his reason or commonsense[138] to the promise will be scandalized by the hidden wisdom of the cross.[139] Only the humble, who distrust their own powers of reason and sight[140] and who place their confidence in the word of Christ alone,[141] achieve true *intellectus*. They alone discern the spirit hidden underneath the letter.

Luther applies the theme of the hiddenness of God not simply to the work of God in Christ but also to his work in the Church and in the faithful soul. The mystery of the incarnation is the mystery of God hidden in the flesh.[142] God cannot be discerned by sight in Jesus of Nazareth but only by the hearing of faith.[143] The ear is equipped by grace to discern what the eye cannot.

Similarly hiddenness is a category which applies to the Church. Just as in the past the Church was hidden in the synagogue,[144] so now in the present its wisdom and glory are hidden *sub contrario*.[145] Moreover, the

---

134. *WA* 55¹.20.13–15; 3.311.35–36.   135. *WA* 3.127.19–24.

136. *WA* 4.356.9–13; 4.95.1–4. One should be careful not to mistake the contrast between ear and eye as a general preference for auditory over visual learning. John Dillenberger administers a rebuke to any who misread Luther in this way when he remarks: "The apprehension of God in the cross is not a matter of seeing but of having one's eyes opened. It is not a matter of hearing but of having one's ears opened. God is not simply apparent in the cross as other things are apparent to human beings. The perception of God in the cross implies that the form and content of God's communication of himself do not allow man to treat him as other things. God discloses himself to man but the form excludes that he be taken for granted. God gives himself but the content of that gift is still surrounded by mystery. It is no wonder that the cross is foolishness to those who want to know God directly by revelation." John Dillenberger, *God Hidden and Revealed* (Philadelphia: Muhlenberg Press, 1953), p. xiv.

137. *WA* 3.548.2–5.   142. *WA* 4.6.40–7.3; 55².73.29ff.
138. *WA* 3.141.23ff.; 3.548.6–9.   143. *WA* 3.124.33–35.
139. *WA* 4.82.37–83.2.   144. *WA* 3.395.3–4.
140. *WA* 4.83.3–9.   145. *WA* 4.77.35–78.9.
141. *WA* 3.651.19–22.

faith by which the Church lives is also a hidden reality, hidden in its exercise and in its object. The Church does not place its confidence in visible things, but in the "things which do not appear" (*res non apparentes*) which are grasped by faith and cannot yet be seen.[146]

As the Church is regarded as weak and foolish in the eyes of the world, so, too, is the just man, whom the world dismisses with contempt.[147] He is hidden in the Church, because his existence is not determined by what reason approves but by the hidden realities the Church confesses.[148] Even his sanctification is hidden, since the love of God which perfects him is hidden under what appear to be bitter trials.[149] In short, the saving work and revelation of God in Christ, in the Church, and in the faithful soul is a work hidden under contrary appearances.

The theologian who attempts to distinguish letter from spirit must therefore remember that while there are contexts in which one must emphasize the correlation between the sign and the thing signified, there are other contexts in which one must admit a radical disjuncture.[150] Though the law of Moses understood according to the spirit is a sign of the saving act of God in Jesus Christ, that saving act is hidden from sight under the form of a contrary appearance. As faith must hear the promise and perceive the correlation, so, too, it must penetrate the scandal of contrary appearances in the light of that same promise and grasp the hidden revelation. The God of Holy Scripture is a God who *discordat signum a signato*.[151]

God's work is effected in the Church by means of his words. Luther distinguishes three modes of the Word of God: (1) from God the Father in himself and in his saints in glory, (2) in his saints in this life in the Spirit, and (3) through an external word directed toward human ears.[152] He relates these modes to three stages of revelation: (1) by the prophets and fathers, (2) in his Son, and (3) in glory face to face.[153] The Word of God is the power by which God creates and redeems. Luther can even affirm that the "works of God are his words."[154]

While Luther exalts the power of the Word of God and insists that the power lies in the Word and not in us,[155] he is nevertheless deeply concerned with the relationship between the Word of God and human language. Human language is the instrument by which God communicates his living

146. WA 3.150.27ff.
147. WA 3.300.21ff.
148. WA 3.150.16–26.
149. WA 4.355.18–23.
150. WA 4.82.14–21.
151. WA 4.82.14–21.
152. WA 3.262.6–9.
153. WA 3.262.10–29.
154. WA 3.152.5–8.
155. WA 4.216.40–41.

words to our hearts.[156] Words are the vehicle of the very truth[157] which creates faith.[158] Human language perceived by human ears is the channel which mediates the work of God to faith.[159] As Christ was born from the human body of Mary, so the Church is born from the human language of Scripture.[160] Preaching of these words creates a new possibility of existence in faith where no such possibility existed before.

When the faithful pray to God for his words, Luther observes, it might appear that they are contenting themselves with preliminary rather than with ultimate things—with the *signa rerum* (the symbols which signify a reality but which are not identical with it) rather than with the *res ipsae* (the ultimately real matters intended by the language of Scripture). While perfectly understandable, such a perception of the meaning of this prayer is not accurate. In the words which Christians desire are hidden the very things which do not yet appear but which are promised to faith. Therefore anyone who has the words of God by faith has the reality signified by those words, albeit in a hidden way.[161] To grasp the gospel by faith is to hold the future in the present.

In view of this attitude toward words it is not surprising that Luther modifies the old monastic motto, *nudus nudum Christum sequens*, to *nudus nudum verbum servans*.[162] The faithful soul hungers for the words of God because the "things which do not appear" can be possessed in no other way. The ability to distinguish letter from spirit compels the theologian to recognize not only the correlation between signs and things and their disjuncture *sub contrario*, but also that in certain circumstances the possession of the signs is the possession of the things signified. The last point is not a dominant motif in the *Dictata*, where Luther prefers to distinguish possession in hope (*in spe*) from possession in fact (*in re*), but it is nevertheless a motif which does occur.

2. *Quadriga.* In distinguishing letter from spirit Luther makes use of the Quadriga or fourfold sense of Scripture: literal, allegorical, tropological, and anagogical. When Luther speaks of the literal sense of Scripture, he is not so much interested in the literal-historical meaning of the text (the plain story told by the words) as he is in the literal-prophetic sense (the meaning of the text as it refers to Jesus Christ).[163] The letter is whatever

156. *WA* 3.256.5–11.
157. *WA* 4.229.37–39.
158. *WA* 4.183.21–22.
159. *WA* 3.500.16–19; 4.9.18–19.
160. *WA* 3.454.24–25.
161. *WA* 4.376.13–20.
162. *WA* 4.390.1–5.
163. *WA* 4.305.6–12.

concerns Jesus Christ in his person.[164] The allegorical sense describes his aid to the Church and the tropological his gracious work in the individual Christian. The anagogical sense, which is not separately emphasized by Luther for reasons we shall soon make clear, points ahead toward the completion of the work of God in Christ, in the Church, and in the Christian. All four senses of Scripture find their unity in Christ [165] and the literal-prophetic is basic to the other three.

At the same time that Luther emphasizes the literal-prophetic sense of Scripture, the Word and Deed of Christ in history for human salvation, he stresses with equal force and tenacity the tropological sense, the significance of the Word and Deed of Christ for faith. By tropological Luther does not have in mind the customary reference to the moral sense of Scripture, the *agenda* or deeds to be performed in the power of the justifying love (*caritas*) of God. The tropological "good" (*bonum tropologicum*) is faith, not love.[166] Faith is directed toward the saving act of God in Christ (the literal-prophetic sense of Scripture). From faith the Church is created (the allegorical sense) and through faith the Church is brought to perfection (the anagogical sense). Everyone who has the tropological good of faith lives according to the spirit and not according to the letter. He thus stands in the proper relationship to the text which is to be interpreted and can easily gain a right understanding of it. From the standpoint of the divine initiative and the saving act of God in history, the literal-prophetic sense is basic to the others. From the standpoint of the reception of that act in faith, the tropological sense is fundamental.[167]

Luther does not stress the anagogical sense[168] of Scripture because a future-oriented dynamic shapes the whole of his commentary on the Psalms. The God of Holy Scripture is a God who enters into covenant and who makes promises.[169] He is a faithful God who both can and does fulfill the promises which he extends to his elect people. Indeed, when Scripture speaks of the truth of God, it has in mind not so much the verifiability of dogmatic propositions as the fidelity of God in and to his promises.[170] "Truth," Luther concludes, "is the fulfillment of a promise."[171]

The proper response to a promise is faith. Since, however, promises have

164. *WA* 55¹.8.8–11.
165. *WA* 55².63.10–16.
166. *WA* 3.532.23–26.
167. *WA* 3.531.33–37.
168. Medieval exegesis never was very much interested in anagogy, so that Luther's lack of interest in it is not remarkable in itself. What is important to note, however, are Luther's reasons for his inattention to the anagogical meaning of Scripture.
169. *WA* 4.40.14–15; 3.128.18–21.   171. *WA* 4.245.34–37.
170. *WA* 3.199.16–18; 4.2.20; 4.13.13–27.

largely, though not exclusively, to do with matters that are still pending in the future (*res non apparentes*), faith for Luther has to a great extent the character of hope. That is not to say that faith and hope are synonymous. Faith embraces *intellectus*[172] (understanding the spirit of Scripture), *affectus*[173] (human motivation to obey the Word of God who acts in history for human salvation), and *memoria*[174] (confession of the mighty deeds of God in the past) as well as hope. Nevertheless, to be justified by faith is to live in hope rather than in full possession of the realities promised to faith. Luther can insist that we have all our goods in words and promises[175] and "possess them to the extent that we believe and hope."[176]

The future-oriented character of faith is clarified by Luther's reflections on the meaning of substance. The philosophers are no help in explaining the meaning of substance. Aristotle is concerned with the empirical valuation of visible things.[177] Faith, on the other hand, is directed toward invisible realities, invisible either because they are future or because they are hidden from sight under the form of a contrary appearance.[178] Therefore Aristotle cannot help us when Scripture proposes that "faith is the substance of things hoped for (Heb. 11:1)."[179]

When philosophers talk of substance, they are concerned with the quiddities of things. Scripture, on the contrary, is not concerned with the essence of a thing, but with its qualities. How a person lives in the world and what that person does as he conducts his life are the questions which trouble the biblical writers.[180] The substance of a person, therefore, is not his quiddity or essence. It is rather the foundation or ground on which he stands as he lives and acts. It is the underlying structure from which he lives and on which he depends for the fundamental meaning of his

172. *WA* 3.176.3–10.

173. *WA* 4.356.23–28.

174. *WA* 3.147.3–5; 3.127.18–20.

175. *WA* 4.272.16–26.

176. *WA* 3.180.24–26.

177. *WA* 3.507.34–508.5.

178. Wicks criticizes Hendrix for laying such stress on *fides futurorum* that he omits to mention the importance of *absconditas sub contrario* for Luther: "His account of the new authenticity by way of trust in promised goods gives quite a selective picture of what authentic faith grasps. It is a false modernization to make of Luther a theologian of hope in 1515. He has extensive passages in the *Dictata* in which faith's object is the *opus Dei* now unfolding, but in the paradoxical manner of hiddenness under contrary appearances." *Theological Studies* 36 (1975), p. 186.

179. *WA* 4.168.1. For a sensitive and helpful discussion of what substance means for the young Luther, see especially Steven E. Ozment, *Homo Spiritualis, A Comparative Study of the Anthropology of Johannes Tauler, Jean Gerson, and Martin Luther (1509–16) in the Context of their Theological Thought*, SMRT 6 (Leiden, 1969), pp. 105–9. Cf. *WA* 3.649.17–20.

180. *WA* 3.419.36–420.1.

existence. Whatever one builds one's life upon, that is one's substance.[181] The sinner builds his life on the goods of this world,[182] but the believer on the goods promised to faith, the "things which do not appear."

Christians have no substance in this world except hope.[183] They live by bare expectation (*nuda spe*)[184] and are despised by a world which builds its life on the substantial goods of wealth, power, and success.[185] Sinners live before the world *in re*; that is, the foundation of their lives is tangible, visible, and fully possessed in the present. Christians, on the other hand, live in the sight of other men *in spe*, since all faith can produce on demand are words and promises. Tangibility belongs to the future. As a result the works of God are intelligible in this life "in hope not in fact."[186]

Christian existence is characterized both by hope and by despair. The Christian cannot find his substance in himself any more than he can locate it in the visible goods of this passing world. He must despair of himself[187] and of the moral powers and natural virtues[188] so exalted by Gabriel Biel and the Tübingen nominalists and place his hope and confidence in the words of Christ.[189] The Christian pilgrimage is directed toward the future. We are saved insofar as we have what is promised and are not saved insofar as we still lack what will be granted in the future.[190] The faithful people of God cry out for salvation in the sense that they long to possess in fact what they now possess only by naked hope. Christians may be described as those who possess and are yet to possess the things revealed to faith.[191]

To complicate the matter still more, to the extent that possessions of the signs is possession of the things signified by them the Christian stands at the beginning of his life as one who receives the promise of God and at the end as one who is already saved. Tropological existence is existence in hope. But because that hope is guaranteed by the truth of God—i.e., by his fidelity to his promises which secure their final realization—tropological existence is at the same time anagogical.

The literal-prophetic sense of Scripture centers on Christ, the Truth who fulfills all figures[192] and promises[193] of the Old Testament and who comes to us where we are in order to lead us back to where he is.[194] Luther

181. *WA* 3.419.25–31.
182. *WA* 3.420.2–5.
183. *WA* 3.410.16–19.
184. *WA* 3.410.16–19.
185. *WA* 4.355.29–32.
186. *WA* 4.367.34–39.
187. *WA* 3.453.1–2.

188. *WA* 4.274.20–22.
189. *WA* 4.332.11–12.
190. *WA* 4.375.1–9.
191. *WA* 4.375.1–9.
192. *WA* 4.13.3–5.
193. *WA* 4.13.7–9.
194. *WA* 4.17.34–42.

insists that there are three advents of Jesus Christ: *in carnem, per gratiam,* and *per gloriam*—in the flesh, by grace, and in glory. The advent of Christ in the flesh was anticipated by the saints and prophets of the Old Testament,[195] who read the law of Moses according to the spirit and who belong to the Church which has existed from the very beginning in Adam.[196] The advent in the flesh was hidden from sight, not that Christ lacked the substance of real, human flesh or that he performed his saving acts in secret,[197] but because the presence of God was hidden *sub contrario*.[198]

Christ destroyed the glory of the world through his humility[199] and achieved his victory through defeat.[200] Because he did not come in the pomp of the world like a proper king, he was rejected both by those Jews who were children of Abraham solely according to the flesh and by Gentiles who found their substance quite adequately located in the goods of this present life.[201] The mystery of God hidden in the flesh is only understood by faith. It is anticipated by the faithful synagogue and confessed by the Church. Whoever wishes to find God must find him hidden in the flesh of Jesus of Nazareth. One must proceed from the humanity of Jesus to the mystery of the divine presence underneath and beyond it.[202]

The first advent in the flesh is for the sake of the second advent by grace.[203] Because the work of God in Christ is hidden under the form of its contrary, the revelation of Christ by grace takes place in the believers who hear the proclamation of the word of the apostles.[204] Christ does not come in his spiritual advent to those pious souls who have merited his presence by the exercise of their innate moral powers, nor does he refuse to come to sinners because of their demerits.[205] The spiritual advent is for sinners, who despair of themselves and seek their substance in the word of Christ. The advent of Christ by grace is the point in time at which the literal-prophetic sense becomes the tropological sense and apart from which it remains the bare and deadly *littera occidens*.

The advent by grace, which is accessible solely to hearing, points toward the third advent in glory, which will be visible to the eye.[206] All three ad-

---

195. WA 3.523.21–31.
196. WA 3.494.26–29.
197. WA 4.244.33–39.
198. WA 4.337.10–12.
199. WA 55².102.15–21.
200. WA 3.160.7–11.
201. WA 4.94.25–30.

202. WA 3.141.34–40. Cf. the interesting parallel between Luther's remarks here about the king who is a pauper with Luther's sermon for the first Sunday in Advent, 1533. WA 37.201ff.

203. WA 4.19.31–36; 4.94.32–33.
204. WA 3.625.29–34.
205. WA 4.263.1–13.
206. WA 3.625.29–34.

vents, however, are tightly bound together in Luther's thought, so much so that he lays down the hermeneutical rule for his students that whenever any verse is explained or can be explained with reference to Christ in the flesh, it ought at the same time (*simul*) to be interpreted with reference to his coming in grace and his last advent in glory.[207]

3. *Caput-corpus-membra*. The third and final hermeneutical device employed by Luther is the so-called *caput-corpus-membra* schema. All Scripture is written concerning Christ.[208] Because of the union of Christ and the Church as head and body,[209] whatever is spoken prophetically concerning Christ is at the same time (*simul*) posited of the Church his body and of every member in it.[210] Since head and members form one body—Luther can even say one flesh[211]—transition from the one to the other is relatively easy.[212] There is a second way in which Christ and the Church may be regarded as one flesh; namely, in the spiritual marriage of faith in which Christ is the bridegroom and the Church or individual soul is the bride.[213] This, too, is a hermeneutical consideration, not merely a soteriological one.[214] Still, whether one speaks of head-body-members or of bridegroom and bride, the bond of union which unites Christ with his Church is the bond of faith.[215]

What may be said concerning the head is the literal-prophetic sense of Scripture; what concerning the body, the allegorical; and what concerning the individual soul, the tropological. The advantage of the *caput-corpus-membra* schema over the Quadriga is the way in which it emphasizes the inescapable interconnection between the literal, allegorical, and tropological senses of Scripture and preserves in a striking way the role of the Church as a middle term between Christ and the faithful soul. It is therefore not pointlessly redundant of Luther to make use of it as well as the Quadriga and the distinction between letter and spirit. All three hermeneutical schemata have an important role to play in Luther's thought.

A final motif in Luther's interpretation of the Psalms should be mentioned here, though it will be dealt with more systematically in the next chapter, and that is the theme of the praise of God. Luther has nothing to say about the praise of God in his notes on Augustine and Peter Lombard,

207. *WA* 4.344.7–15.
208. *WA* 55².62.15ff.
209. *WA* 3.254.24–32; 3.131.15–16.
210. *WA* 3.132.21–23; 3.127.30–32.
211. *WA* 3.254.24–32.

212. *WA* 4.275.29–31; 3.212.27–35.
213. *WA* 3.211.23–25.
214. *WA* 3.142.26–30.
215. *WA* 55².105.6–9.

an omission all the more striking because of the prominence of this theme in Staupitz. There is a shift, however, from the early works to the *Dictata*, where the theme of the praise of God with its *duplex confessio,* the confession of praise and of sin, becomes an important motif.[216] The new man, who has received the spiritual advent of Christ in faith, sings the new song of the praise of God.[217] What Luther means by this can be better explained in the context of justification than in the context of hermeneutics. Nevertheless, it deserves to be mentioned in the context of hermeneutics that Luther now regards the confession of the praise of God to be the noblest work of man.[218]

III. *Conclusion*

The conclusion to which a historian is forced after reading and comparing Luther and Staupitz on the Old Testament is that, in spite of certain similarities at specific points, the hermeneutical approach of the two theologians is strikingly different. To be sure, both Luther and Staupitz cite the *Enarrationes in psalmos* with great regularity, both make use of the *caput-corpus-membra* schema, both avoid scholastic disputations on the text, both regard the New Testament as the hermeneutical key which unlocks the Old, and both define the highest task of the Christian as the confession of the praise of God. There is, however, nothing unique to Staupitz's theology in this list of agreements. These themes are common enough in the medieval theological and exegetical tradition. There is no reason, therefore, to believe that the appearance of these hermeneutical motifs in the biblical interpretation of Martin Luther is a direct result of the influence of John Staupitz.

The differences are more than merely superficial. It is not simply that Staupitz lacks Hebrew and makes no use of late medieval commentaries or that one can find no reference to the Quadriga and the literal-prophetic sense in his reflections on Job. Nor is it the fact that Staupitz writes short doctrinal and moral treatises on topics suggested by the text while Luther concentrates his attention more directly on the work of exegesis. Not even the difference in their attitude toward Aristotle and the metaphysicians marks the boundary which separates them.

216. *WA* 4.238.14–21.   218. *WA* 3.262.2–4.
217. *WA* 3.182.24–27.

What divides them, more than anything else, is Luther's developing conception of faith. Faith is the tropological good. Its correlation with the promises of God testifies to "the things which do not appear," realities which are invisible because they are future or because they are hidden in the present under the form of a contrary appearance. There is nothing in Staupitz's theology which even closely approximates Luther's new understanding of faith and promise. The christological concentration which is characteristic of Luther's thought finds an echo in Staupitz's later writings but no parallel in the sermons on Job.

Staupitz's theology is oriented around love rather than around faith and hope. The Christian is justified, not by faith in a promise which is a witness to invisible realities, but by the communication of grace through the sacraments of the Church. Luther, of course, does not deny the reality of sacramental grace, but it becomes increasingly marginal to his thought in the *Dictata*. For Luther the Christian is one who strains toward the future and who stands in a dialectical relationship to the present.

This difference in the understanding of the nature and role of faith leads to a different vision of the history of salvation. Staupitz writes sapiential theology as he attempts to unfold in an objective manner a drama which begins with the pretemporal decrees of providence and predestination. The past—if one can speak of an eternal decree as past—is the key to the present. History is the plain, straightforward, step-by-step execution in time of decisions made in and by God. The future will unfold, as the past and present have before it, according to exemplars in the mind of God. The future is not a problem, but neither is it a source of consolation or of hope. Staupitz is, in a word, not future-oriented. When he feels the need of consolation, he meditates on the past event of the cross or rejoices in the present possession of grace. The future receives hardly any attention at all.

While Luther is not exclusively oriented toward the future in his lectures on the Psalms, his use of "sign," "promise," "testimony," "shadow," "bare hope," "substance," and "expectation" point strongly in that direction. Luther does not gladly ponder eternal decrees. He begins with the existential situation of Christ, the Church, and the believer. Even the past is interpreted in such a way as to emphasize that it, too, once was future. The cross and resurrection are *res*, but they are realities for which the law of Moses and the writings of the prophets were *signa*. The faithful synagogue was marked by its expectant longing for the saving act of God in the *res non apparentes* of the cross and resurrection of Jesus. Luther begins, when he can, with the human situation before God and describes the event of faith in the historical context of promise and fulfillment. That may not offer a grand enough prospect for more ambitious theologians who chafe and grow irritable when they cannot speculate about the pretemporal counsels of God, but it is all the prospect Luther wants.

Bauer's contention, that Luther derived his early hermeneutic from Staupitz, cannot be sustained. If Luther had remained within the hermeneutical framework utilized by Staupitz, he would have written an altogether different kind of commentary, one which would have placed the Psalms in the context of the divine decrees rather than in the context of the divine promises. It is undoubtedly the case that Staupitz could have commented on the Psalms following those principles. It is, I think, beyond dispute that Luther did not.

III. HUMILITY AND JUSTIFICATION

In 1958 Ernst Bizer[1] startled the relatively quiet world of Reformation scholarship by challenging the prevailing view of Luther's early theological development. According to the historians who had dominated the field of Luther interpretation since Karl Holl, Luther's sudden insight into the meaning of Romans 1:17 and his decisive break with the medieval understanding of the righteousness of God occurred fairly early, probably during his first lectures on the Psalms, certainly before his lectures on Romans.[2] Erich Vogelsang[3] and Emmanuel Hirsch[4] were even bold enough to designate the very Psalm on which Luther was lecturing when his theological world shifted, though they were unable to agree with each other over which Psalm to name.[5]

To be sure, the consensus was not unanimous. Historians like Hartmann Grisar[6] and Carl Stange[7] had argued for a relatively late date for Luther's theological reorientation. A. V. Mueller,[8] eccentric as always, located the transition in Luther's thought during his lectures on Romans. Uuras Saarnivaara[9] placed Luther's discovery of the central message of St. Paul at the end of the year 1518, though one could detect behind Saarnivaara's historical arguments an orthodox Lutheran polemic against the Ritschlian presuppositions of the school of Karl Holl. But these were exceptions in what was, on the whole, a fairly solid front. Historians might differ whether Luther's break with his medieval past took place in 1512 or 1514, but they were serenely confident it had occurred prior to 1516.

1. Ernst Bizer, *Fides ex auditu*, second rev. ed. (Neukirchen Kreis Moers, 1961).
2. For a comprehensive survey of German scholarship on the young Luther, see Kenneth G. Hagen, "Changes in the Understanding of Luther: The Development of the Young Luther," *Theological Studies* 29 (1968): 472–96.
3. Erich Vogelsang, *Die Anfänge von Luthers Christologie nach der ersten Psalmenvorlesung*, AKG 15 (Berlin and Leipzig, 1929).
4. Emanuel Hirsch, "Initium Theologiae Lutheri," in *Lutherstudien II* (Gütersloh, 1954), pp. 9–35.
5. Vogelsang found the decisive turning point in Luther's exegesis of Psalm 71:2. Cf. *Anfänge*, pp. 57–61. Hirsch, on the other hand, designated the exegesis of Psalm 31:2 as the crucial moment in the development of the young Luther. Cf. "Initium," pp. 27–33.
6. Hartmann Grisar, S.J., *Luther* (Freiburg, 1911), 1:50.
7. Carl Stange, *Die Anfänge der Theologie Luthers* (Berlin, 1957), pp. 10ff.
8. Alphons Victor Mueller, *Luthers Werdegang bis zum Turmerlebnis* (Gotha, 1920), pp. 122, 136.
9. Uuras Saarnivaara, *Luther Discovers the Gospel* (St. Louis: Concordia Publishing House, 1951), pp. 92–120.

Bizer's challenge to that consensus in his book, *Fides ex auditu*, was particularly unwelcome. According to Bizer, who located the transition in Luther's thought in the winter of 1517–18,[10] one could run a divining rod over the whole of the *Dictata super Psalterium* without finding a trace of the new theology of the Reformation. In 1513 Luther understood the righteousness of God in severe terms as the activity of a just God who accuses and punishes sinners.[11] By humiliating sinners, God creates in them the humility which is their sole righteousness before God. When Luther speaks of faith in this early commentary as he does with almost embarrassing frequency, he has nothing more revolutionary in mind than the old monastic virtue of humility.[12]

By the end of the decade all this changes decisively.[13] In 1518 Luther is recommending faith as trust in the Word of God. This new understanding of faith is linked to an equally new understanding of the Word of God, particularly the preached Word, as the means of grace which justifies the sinner. But in the first lectures on the Psalms the talk is all of humility, self-accusation, judgment, and the frame of reference is no wider than the cloister walls. Luther's message in 1514 is that the way of humiliation is the way of salvation, because it is to the humble that God gives his grace.[14] By 1518 he has left that essentially monastic message behind and is preaching a radically new theology of Word and faith.

Not only was Bizer frankly unimpressed with the level of Luther's theological insight in the *Dictata*, but he found no reason to regard it as particularly original. John Staupitz had taught much the same thing[15] and it

10. Bizer, *Fides ex auditu*, p. 165: "Nach allem bisher Gesagten scheint unbestreitbar zu sein, daß sich vom Winter 1517 ab eine einschneidende Veränderung in der Theologie Luthers vollzogen hat."

11. Bizer, *Fides ex auditu*, p. 22; "Er versteht die Gerechtigkeit Gottes als anklagende und strafende Gerechtigkeit, als anklagendes Wirken Gottes, das dann allerdings in uns die Demut als die neue Gerechtigkeit wirkt."

12. Bizer, *Fides ex auditu*, p. 20: "Fides ist nur ein anderer Ausdruck für humilitas."

13. Bizer, *Fides ex auditu*, p. 167: "Was Luther entdeckt hat, ist zunächst die Theologie des Wortes und *im Zusammenhang* damit die Bedeutung des Glaubens. Das Wort zeigt nicht einfach den Weg zur Gerechtigkeit und beschreibt diesen nicht nur, sondern es ist das Mittel, wodurch Gott den Menschen rechtfertigt, weil es den Glauben weckt."

14. Bizer, *Fides ex auditu*, p. 22: "Iudicium und Iustitia sind tropologisch als Demut zu verstehen, und diese kann als fides Christi verstanden werden, denn auch Christus hat sich gedemütigt. Damit scheint Röm. 1, 17 Genüge getan. Als eine Folge der Demütigung durch Gott ist diese Demut nicht unser eigenes Werk. Sie erfüllt das Gesetz, weil sie das Sterben des alten Menschen bedeutet."

15. Bizer, *Fides ex auditu*, p. 19: "Es klingt wie eine weitere Ausführung dieses Gedankens, wenn Staupitz sagt, Demut, Gehorsam und Geduld müsse man bei Christus am Kreuz holen, und durch die Demut werde der Mensch dann gerechtfertigt."

was only natural that Luther would echo themes and ideas from the teaching of a man to whom he felt deeply indebted. At any rate, whether Luther consciously followed Staupitz or not, it is indisputable that all the essential elements of his early piety are found in the sermons and tabletalk of Staupitz.

Bizer's sortie against the received teaching of the principal Reformation historians in Europe provoked a fierce and aggressive counterattack. Heinrich Bornkamm in his article, "Zur Frage der Iustitia Dei beim jungen Luther,"[16] and Regin Prenter in his book, *Der barmherzige Richter*,[17] sharply dissented from Bizer's method and conclusions. Bornkamm grumbled that Bizer had not dealt with the whole of the *Dictata* but had narrowly limited his discussion to Psalm 71 (72):2, the verse in which Erich Vogelsang had claimed to find Luther's new understanding of the righteousness of God.[18] Bizer's treatment of Luther's lectures on Romans was no better. No one with any historical or theological acumen could seriously study Luther's comments on Romans 3:22, 4:7, 7:17, 7:25, or 10:6 and detect any disagreement whatever in them with Luther's later theology.[19] Indeed, Prenter and Bornkamm concurred that while it is true that humility is in some sense equivalent to faith in Luther's earliest thought, one should not understand by this formula that faith is nothing more than the monastic virtue of humility (as Bizer argued), but rather that humility must be redefined in terms of Luther's new understanding of faith.[20]

In his *Antrittsvorlesung*[21] at the University of Tübingen, Heiko Oberman drew a distinction between three kinds of humility: (1) the monastic virtue, which in Oberman's opinion is not what Luther had in mind in the

Cf. p. 20: "Die Grundgedanken finden sich nicht weniger bei Staupitz als bei Luther." See also p. 22: "Alle wesentlichen Züge der Frömmigkeit sind bereit bei Staupitz zu finden."

16. Heinrich Bornkamm, "Zur Frage der Iustitia Dei beim jungen Luther," *ARG* 52 (1961): 16–29; *ARG* 53 (1962): 1–60.

17. Regin Prenter, *Der barmherzige Richter* (Copenhagen, 1961).

18. Bornkamm, "Zur Frage," *ARG* 52 (1961): 19–29.

19. Bornkamm, "Zur Frage," *ARG* 53 (1962): 1–25.

20. Bornkamm quotes with approval the words of Gerhard Ebeling, "Gerade die Heranziehung des humilitas-Begriffs dient zur Uminterpretation des traditionellen Verständnisses des Glaubens als eines habitus des Intellekts zu einem den ganzen Menschen betreffenden passiven Geschehen." "Zur Frage," *ARG* 53 (1962): 57. Prenter agrees that Luther's early theology of humility excludes synergism and comes to the conclusion in *Der barmherzige Richter*, p. 77, that: "So stehen wir hier vor der 'echten Humilitastheologie' Luthers, die kein Gegensatz zu seiner 'Glaubenstheologie' bildet, sondern ihr echter Ausdruck ist."

21. Heiko A. Oberman, "Wir sein pettler. Hoc est verum, Bund und Gnade in der Theologie des Mittelalters und der Reformation," *ZKG* 78 (1967): 232–52.

Dictata; (2) humility as Luther explained it in his early writings on the Psalms and Romans; and (3) humility as Luther understood it throughout his life until his confession on his deathbed, "Wir sein Bettler: Hoc est verum."²² As Oberman reads the relevant texts, humility is not a virtue, but the confession that the sinner stands in the presence of God with empty hands and seeks his salvation outside himself.²³ The Christian is a beggar, who can do nothing except cry out for the salvation found in Christ.²⁴ By understanding humility in this way Luther went beyond the teaching of his friend Staupitz, who presupposed the necessity of prevenient grace for the proper disposition for the reception of justifying grace, but who never reduced that disposition to a mere cry (*clamare*). While Luther is a theologian of humility, he means by humility something other than the old monastic virtue, something more radical even than the teaching of Staupitz.²⁵

There the debate stands at the moment. What does Luther mean by humility and to what extent does he agree with Staupitz? Is Luther's doctrine of justification in the *Dictata super Psalterium* virtually the same as Staupitz's doctrine in his sermons on Job? To answer this question we must restrict ourselves, as Bizer did not, to works of Luther and Staupitz written prior to 1516.²⁶ For Staupitz that includes his *Nachfolgung des willigens sterbens Christi* as well as his sermons on Job; for Luther it implies primarily the *Dictata*.

1. Humility and Justification in the Early Writings of John Staupitz (1497–1515)

The sermons on Job are more remarkable for their orthodoxy than for their originality. They offer the sound, old Augustinian solutions to the

22. Oberman, "Wir sein pettler," p. 234.
23. Oberman, "Wir sein pettler," p. 240–42.
24. Oberman, "Wir sein pettler," p. 250.
25. Cf. Oberman, "Wir sein pettler," p. 250: "Die durch den Bund geforderte humilitas ist somit keine irgendwie geartete Tugend; sie ist vielmehr die Anerkennung der Bedürftigkeit und Haltlosigkeit des Menschen."
26. Bizer draws his conclusions by comparing materials from Staupitz's German writings of 1517 with the theology of Luther in 1513–15. He does not work through the early writings of Staupitz, particularly the sermons on Job, but relies on the work of Ernst Wolf. Cf. *Fides ex auditu*, pp. 49–50. I find myself in agreement with Bornkamm's criticism of Bizer's use of Staupitz when Bornkamm observes: "Staupitz ist der einzige, den Bizer gelegentlich zum Vergleich und zum Erweis vorreformatorischen Denkens bei Luther herangezogen hat. Aber die von ihm angeführten Texte besagen dafür nichts," "Zur Frage," p. 54, footnote 238.

problems of nature and grace which had been offered before. Certainly, the reader does not come away from these sermons with the impression (which is unavoidable in the case of Staupitz's later treatise on predestination) that he has been in touch with a creative and original mind.

The chief end of human existence, according to the sermons on Job, is the praise of God.[27] While the world may be used (*uti*) and to that extent loved, only God may be enjoyed (*frui*) as the final goal of human longing.[28] Good as creation is (and Staupitz entertains no doubt that it is very good indeed), it can never promise human nature its ultimate fulfillment.[29] Human life finds its fruition in the love and praise of God or it does not find it at all.[30]

Staupitz conceives of the human predicament in radically Augustinian terms. Pride[31] is the ground of man's alienation from God and self-love[32] is its fundamental principle. As a sinner man uses God and seeks his final end in the created order, precisely where it can never be found.[33] While the sinner still desires the highest good,[34] he does not remember who or what that highest good may be[35] and is therefore utterly incapable of reaching the object of his restless quest for meaning. The whole nature of fallen man is utterly infirm.[36] Staupitz exhausts the full range of the Augustinian vocabulary when he bleakly describes sin as non-being,[37] pride,[38] self-love,[39] disobedience,[40] and impenitence.[41]

The presupposition for human redemption is absolute and unconditional predestination. Justification is the execution in time of an eternal decree of election. No one can be saved, therefore, who is not elect.[42] In fact, Staupitz lays such heavy stress on predestination that he appears to regard the relationship of God to the world as a kind of one-sided covenant. Moved only by his mercy and not, as Anselm had mistakenly believed, by his justice,[43] God has determined to give his grace to the elect apart from any consideration of their merit or demerit. Staupitz is not even willing to qualify predestination, as Alexander of Hales had done, by appeal-

27. *Hiob* 1.3.8–10; 2.11.17–24; 5.27.8–10; 5.32.26–33; 7.44.36–37; 8.56.14–22; 30.229.2–4; and also 7.44.41–45.3.
28. *Hiob* 6.35.10–14.
29. *Hiob* 18.152.41–153.11. Cf. 6.33.26–28.   36. *Hiob* 12.104.14–18.
30. *Hiob* 18.153.19–21.   37. *Hiob* 23.184.4–6.
31. *Hiob* 7.51.12–14.   38. *Hiob* 7.51.12–14.
32. *Hiob* 24.194.24–30.   39. *Hiob* 24.194.24–30.
33. *Hiob* 25.199.29–32.   40. *Hiob* 25.199.16–19; 13.121.31–35.
34. *Hiob* 4.24.25–28.   41. *Hiob* 12.105.17–26.
35. *Hiob* 9.70.16–21.   42. *Hiob* 11.92.6–22.
43. *Hiob* 9.70.36–38; 11.88.34–41; 12.104.18–20; 12.107.32–36.

ing to the foreknown use of grace. Election is a sacred mystery and any attempt to reduce it to simple rational intelligibility will founder in the boundless ocean of the secret counsels of God.

With such a strong view of predestination, it is surprising to find Staupitz elsewhere in his sermons advising sinners to prepare themselves for the reception of justifying grace by doing what is in them (facere quod in se est).[44] But the puzzlement dissolves when Staupitz clarifies what he means. Free will cannot dispose itself for the reception of justifying grace apart from the external action of God in preaching,[45] temptation,[46] and the sacraments,[47] and an interior renewal by the Holy Spirit.[48] "Doing what is in one" does not imply for Staupitz that the sinner is able to perform works which are meritorious, not even in the sense of merits of congruity, since the good works of the sinner are not, properly speaking, morally good.[49] God begins his work of renewal by instilling humility in the sinner, by convincing him he cannot trust his own righteousness but must seek his salvation in God alone. The sinner who judges himself before he is judged by God is the sinner who will be justified.[50]

There is a sense in which, by retaining the language of "doing what is in one," Staupitz has retained the language of a two-sided covenant. It is the language of do ut des, of contracts negotiated and bargains struck. God will give his grace to people who do something. But when one examines what it is that sinners are expected to do in order to receive God's grace, it is clear that the language is more than a little misleading. "To do what is in one" is to struggle against sin, to accuse oneself as a sinner, to abandon all hope of making oneself righteous before God by one's own pious acts.[51] Humility is not a virtue which the sinner offers to God in exchange for grace, but an embarrassed confession that the sinner has nothing whatever to exchange but his own sin. Goodness and dignity are found in God alone.[52]

Furthermore, humility can find no Dickensian grounds for pride in its own demerit and powerlessness. Humility is itself a fruit of predestination.[53] The ability to accuse oneself is not a natural but, to use the expres-

44. Hiob 23.189.6–23.
45. Hiob 19.162.7–10; 19.162.28–30; cf. 11.94.33–34; 12.101.8–9.
46. Hiob 1.3.11–17.   49. Hiob 23.186.39–187.3; 23.189.6–23.
47. Hiob 3.17.23–25.   50. Hiob 22.178.2–9.
48. Hiob 12.114.21–28.   51. Hiob 5.32.13–24.
52. Hiob 1.3.5–24; 23.187.5–8; 23.186.32–187.3.
53. Staupitz's introduction of the subject of accusatio sui and his reflections on the text that judgment must begin at the house of God (11.92.30ff.) follow his discussion

sion of the later Wesleyan theologians, "a gracious ability." In his natural
state the sinner is woefully deficient in self-knowledge.[54] Even his first
dim prehension that all is not well is an effect of the unmerited favor of
God. Nothing could be further from Staupitz's mind than the moral op-
timism of Gabriel Biel or the popular notion that monastic asceticism and
self-renunciation merit God's blessing.

Justifying grace is given to the sinner through the sacraments of the
Church[55] and is described both as a habit of love (*gratia creata*)[56] and as
the Holy Spirit (*gratia increata*).[57] Priority, however, belongs to uncreated
grace. It is the Holy Spirit who moves Christians to perform good works
and who freely accepts them when they are completed.[58] The dignity or
religious value of works produced in cooperation with the habit of grace
rests on divine acceptation.[59] Justification embraces the gift of love and the
nonimputation of sin.[60] It is the restoration of the ability to engage in the
praise of God.

The gift of the Holy Spirit in justification makes possible a life of conformity to Christ, a conformity perceived principally as a union of wills
rather than as an identity of metaphysical substance.[61] Staupitz can also
describe justification as a spiritual marriage or use the analogy of head
and members as a metaphor to explain the relation of Christ, the Church,
and the faithful soul. The spiritual marriage[62] and the *caput-corpus-
membra* schema[63] serve as the basis for an exchange of sin and righteousness between Christ and the Christian to which Staupitz alludes in his
sermons on Job and which he later elaborates in his treatise on predestination.

Temptation is important in the Christian life.[64] While every temptation
can be overcome by resignation to the will of God,[65] the process of temptation is essential as a means of sanctification[66] and as a ground for certi-

---

of *predestinatio* (11.91.27ff.). The progress of the *viator* toward the heavenly Jerusalem
has been foreordained by God in every detail (11.84.19–23).

54. Staupitz emphasizes the importance of preaching in making the sinner aware
of his predicament and recalling him to trust in the mercy of God. *Hiob* 20.169.1–9;
23.188.11–15. Cf. 22.178.2–5.

55. *Hiob* 11.94.15–19, 23.189.23–26; cf. 1.3.11–22; 27.211.17–27.

56. *Hiob* 24.197.27–28.   58. *Hiob* 23.189.23–26.

57. *Hiob* 30.232.17–22; 23.189.3–6.   59. *Hiob* 23.186.32–187.3.

60. *Hiob* 12.113.19–24; 21.171.30–32; 23.187.28–30; 23.187.34–188.9.

61. *Hiob* 3.16.14–18; 3.12.31–39; 3.15.1–3; 3.15.29–31; 24.196.14–22; 24.196.38–197.6.

62. *Hiob* 1.3.29–31; 2.8.7–9.   65. *Hiob* 22.177.12–23.

63. *Hiob* 32.243.25ff.   66. *Hiob* 3.17.23–25.

64. *Hiob* 11.86.28–30; 24.196.8–13.

tude.[67] Testing confirms faith and makes the elect confident of the final salvation for which they hope. Indeed, the truest sign of election is conformity to Christ in undeserved suffering.[68]

Staupitz's reflections on justification in the sermons on Job are supplemented in 1515 by a German treatise on the Christian life entitled *Ein büchlein von der nachfolgung des willigens sterbens Christi*. The book contains a long anthropological essay which defines human existence not merely in terms of its biological or metaphysical character (*sein*) but also in terms of its health and moral integrity (*recht sein*).[69] Death is not merely the loss of one's life, dreadful as that undoubtedly is, but the loss of one's moral integrity, which is far worse. Sinners who have lost their integrity suffer the death of the soul as well as the death of the body.[70]

Staupitz lists seven results of Adam's sin. They make fairly grim reading: inborn sin, stubbornness of the flesh, necessity of dying, the bitterness of death, weakness to do what is good, lack of ability to judge the truth, and covetousness for evil.[71] While man in his original state was still capable of expressing unhindered love for God and neighbor,[72] disobedience made him vulnerable to a threefold death:[73] (1) even though he continues to breathe, his loss of moral integrity constitutes the death of his soul; (2) eventually his body will undergo biological death as a delayed consequence of his sin; and (3) finally both body and soul will be condemned to the everlasting punishment of eternal death.

After such a dismal recital it is almost anticlimactic to observe that Staupitz regards the predicament of the sinner as absolute. He is no longer master of his own disobedient members.[74] His own best efforts go awry and bring down further calamities upon his head.[75] "Dead in trespasses and sins" is a biblical phrase with awesome meaning for Staupitz.

In the midst of his predicament the sinner dare not yield to the temptation to trust his own good works as the ground for regaining the favor of God.[76] There are two reasons why Staupitz warns against self-trust. The first is implied in the description of the predicament. All human righteousness is impure and incapable of withstanding scrutiny by One who is Goodness itself.[77]

67. *Hiob* 27.215.34–35.
68. *Hiob* 11.92.6–22.
69. *Nachfolgung*, Kn. 57.
70. *Nachfolgung*, Kn. 53–54, 58.
71. *Nachfolgung*, Kn. 54–55.
72. *Nachfolgung*, Kn. 52.

73. *Nachfolgung*, Kn. 53–54.
74. *Nachfolgung*, Kn. 56.
75. *Nachfolgung*, Kn. 54.
76. *Nachfolgung*, Kn. 86.
77. *Nachfolgung*, Kn. 69–70.

But the second reason cuts more deeply. Human righteousness is irrelevant as the ground of justification. God does not promise his grace to the righteous but only to sinners.[78] The logical precondition for the presence of God's righteousness is the absence of human merit. Christ alone is the ground for the justification of the sinner.[79] To trust one's own virtue and attempt to offer it to God in exchange for his mercy can only be read as an attempt to be wiser than God.[80] But sinners do not set the terms for God's mercy; God does.[81] And he gives righteousness to the undeserving.

Since the essence of man is not mere *sein* but *recht sein*, a new birth is necessary for man to regain his true nature, the moral integrity lost in the fall.[82] The soul of the Christian is passive in the new birth.[83] Staupitz does not speak of "doing what is in one," not even in the minimal form in which it appears in the sermons on Job. Rather the talk is of suffering something to be done to oneself. There is no room in Staupitz's theology for the notion that one merits the new birth by exemplary acts of moral heroism.[84]

While Staupitz joins with Thomas Aquinas in denying all possibility of meriting grace to sinners, he does not exclude merit altogether from the Christian life. The later Protestants do exclude merit, but Augustine does not and Staupitz has no reason to feel dissatisfied with Augustine's position. Of course, the fact that works are in any sense meritorious can only be cited as further evidence of the grace and patience of God.[85] When God rewards the good works of Christians, he is only setting an additional seal of approval on the work of grace which he is carrying out in them.

Highest merit belongs to men and women who are more concerned to justify Christ *(Christum rechtfertigen)* than to excuse themselves for their own failures.[86] The idea of the justification of God, so important to Luther in his lectures on the Psalms, is an integral part of Staupitz's argument in this treatise. Indeed, the proper form of the Christian life is to justify God alone *(got allein rechtfertiget)* and accuse and condemn oneself *(sich selb vordempt, selb vornichtet)*.[87] If one were to translate Staupitz's remarks on this subject into Latin terminology, one could say that *accusatio sui* and *Deum iustificare* are roughly synonymous.

The death of death is effected by the perfect resignation *(gelassenheit)*

78. *Nachfolgung,* Kn. 86.
79. *Nachfolgung,* Kn. 58–59.
80. *Nachfolgung,* Kn. 86.
81. *Nachfolgung,* Kn. 58.
82. *Nachfolgung,* Kn. 57.

83. *Nachfolgung,* Kn. 78.
84. *Nachfolgung,* Kn. 84.
85. *Nachfolgung,* Kn. 84.
86. *Nachfolgung,* Kn. 71.
87. *Nachfolgung,* Kn. 71.

of Jesus Christ to the will of his Father. Staupitz interprets the *kenosis* of the Son as *Gelassenheit* or resignation.[88] The resignation of the Son was, Staupitz believes, entirely unique.[89] He was not simply resigned (*gelassen*) to the will of God, a resignation which involved the abandonment of all lesser values in order to cling to the will of God alone. He was also abandoned (*verlassen*) by God to death on the cross. He was abandoned that the elect might not be, who follow the example of his resignation.[90] The humility which condemns itself and justifies God in his judgment may also be described as resignation. Those who are perfectly conformed to the mind of God are one will,[91] one spirit,[92] one flesh[93] with Christ.

The resignation of the Christian is a response to the resignation of Jesus Christ.[94] Conformity to the will of God involves the imitation of Christ alone.[95] Staupitz has no interest himself, though he does not proscribe it for others, in modeling his life on the pattern of the saints.[96] This intensive focus on conformity to Christ to the exclusion of the saints represents a shift from the position taken in the earlier sermons on Job. It is enough for Staupitz if he can embrace the motto *nudus nudum Christum sequens* or, as Staupitz frames it in German, *dem nackenden, dem blossen Jesu nackendt und bloss nachfolgen*.[97]

Discipleship is not an activity of individual Christians in isolation from each other. Staupitz agrees with the dictum of John Wesley that the Bible knows nothing of solitary Christianity. To some extent Staupitz's ecclesiological observations are embedded in his Mariological affirmations, where they are not so easy for the untrained eye to detect. Mary, whose identification with the Church is a commonplace of late medieval thought, is the wife and mother of God[98] and, as such, is the mother of the faithful. No one can be a child of Christ who is not a child of Mary.[99] Mariological language, however, is not the only language which Staupitz uses in order to describe the role of the Church. He calls attention to the role of the Church as the environment of grace by explicit and unambiguous statements. The Christian receives the gifts of God in the Church and pleases God so long as he remains in it. Cyprian's judgment that there is no salva-

88. *Nachfolgung*, Kn. 80–81.
89. *Nachfolgung*, Kn. 81.
90. *Nachfolgung*, Kn. 81.
91. *Nachfolgung*, Kn. 82.
92. *Nachfolgung*, Kn. 79.
93. *Nachfolgung*, Kn. 59.
94. *Nachfolgung*, Kn. 81.
95. *Nachfolgung*, Kn. 62.
96. *Nachfolgung*, Kn. 62.
97. *Nachfolgung*, Kn. 72.
98. *Nachfolgung*, Kn. 77.
99. *Nachfolgung*, Kn. 77–78.

tion outside the Church is echoed in the words of Staupitz, *ausserhalb welcher dir nichts gefelt*.[100]

Staupitz composes a long section on temptation in which he lists nine dangerous trials recorded in Luke's gospel: unrepented sin,[101] trust in one's own works,[102] doubt concerning the righteousness of God,[103] care for the souls of others but carelessness with respect to one's own destiny,[104] the conviction that the sinner cannot be made whole and again do what is right,[105] the refusal to believe that Christ is the Son of God,[106] presumptuous trust in the mercy of God,[107] inquisitiveness concerning election,[108] and anxiety that one is not elect.[109] All of these temptations, some of which clearly had been undergone by Luther, may be overcome in the power of God.[110] Christ, whose temptations were far greater than ours,[111] stands ready to assist us through any crisis. The point, of course, at which temptation is most intense is at the moment of death.[112] Staupitz therefore ends his treatise with a few observations on the *ars moriendi*.

11. *Humility and Justification in Luther (1509–15)*

Luther operates, as the preceding chapter has attempted to make clear, with a theological framework which differs in certain important respects from the viewpoint of his friend and superior, Dr. Staupitz. Whereas Staupitz grounds his theological observations in the eternal decrees of providence and predestination, Luther describes the work of God within the historical context of promise and fulfillment. Nevertheless, in spite of the differences in orientation, there are notable similarities in their theological positions.

Perhaps most striking of all in the *Dictata* is the emphasis Luther now gives to the theme of the praise of God. Like Staupitz, Luther believes that the highest work of man is the praise of God.[113] Indeed, since God lacks nothing else which we have, praise is the only thing which we can render to him.[114] Whatever words of gratitude we mumble when overtaken by beauty or joy are owed to God alone and we defraud him of his glory

100. *Nachfolgung*, Kn. 84.
101. *Nachfolgung*, Kn. 63–64.
102. *Nachfolgung*, Kn. 64.
103. *Nachfolgung*, Kn. 64.
104. *Nachfolgung*, Kn. 64–65.
105. *Nachfolgung*, Kn. 65.
106. *Nachfolgung*, Kn. 65.
107. *Nachfolgung*, Kn. 66.
108. *Nachfolgung*, Kn. 66.
109. *Nachfolgung*, Kn. 66.
110. *Nachfolgung*, Kn. 66. Cf. Kn. 63.
111. *Nachfolgung*, Kn. 63.
112. *Nachfolgung*, Kn. 68.
113. *WA* 3.262.2–4; 3.452.20–25.
114. *WA* 3.641.7–9; 3.648.4ff.; 3.372.5–6; 3.210.36–41.

when we deny him that praise and confer it on creatures.[115] The praise of God and the acknowledgment of truth are bound tightly together in Luther's mind. Whenever we speak what is wise or true or good, we give honor to God, since God is Wisdom, Truth, and Goodness itself.[116]

There are preconditions, however, for joining in this song of praise. The renewed song of praise can only be sung by people who have been themselves renewed by grace.[117] The old man, still comfortably locked in his sins, has no disposition to lift up a canticle of praise. The disposition and the ability to sing the new song are only found in the Church.[118] Luther is adamant in his insistence that there is no praise of God outside the Church.[119] In order to praise God, one must displease oneself and take pleasure in God alone.[120] The sinner, who conforms his life to the tastes and norms of the world and who locates his substance in the ends and activities of which other men approve, pleases himself and finds the message of the cross distasteful. The praise of God, granted the hard fact of sin, presupposes self-accusation and an unsparing confession of sin.

Luther talks about a dual or *duplex* confession: the confession of sin and the confession of praise. The two acts of confession imply and require each other.[121] Confession of sin without confession of praise is characteristic of the despair of a convict on the gallows, while confession of praise without confession of sin is pharisaical and leads to religious hypocrisy. One cannot be separated from the other without doing irreparable damage to both. That is not to say that confession of praise and confession of sin are in all respects equal to each other. The confession of praise is clearly the better—one might even say, the worthier—part of the *duplex confessio.*[122]

From time to time Luther speaks of the confession of sin as though it were the precondition for the confession of the praise of God. On other occasions he indicates that the praise of God and remorse for one's sin take place at the same time (*simul laudare deum et gemere peccata nostra*)[123] or simply affirms that the confession of sin is (*est*) the praise of God.[124] The common element in the confession of praise and the confession of sin is the sinner's acknowledgment of the truth. By praising God (*active*) and condemning oneself, the renewed sinner receives praise in

115. *WA* 3.280.23–24; 3.282.23ff.
116. *WA* 3.189.12–14.
117. *WA* 3.182.24–27.
118. *WA* 4.239.20–21.
119. *WA* 3.237.36–38.

120. *WA* 3.191.1–9.
121. *WA* 4.109.18–22; 4.238.14–21.
122. *WA* 4.239.1–3.
123. *WA* 3.644.34–38.
124. *WA* 3.185.6–7; 3.284.37ff.

God (*passive*).[125] In each instance truth is served and the reality of the human situation is openly admitted.

A parallel case is developed when Luther uses the terms self-accusation (*accusatio sui*) and the justification of God (*Deum iustificare*). Luther can talk as if self-accusation were the presupposition for justification.[126] Only those people who abhor their own sin are prepared to receive the gift of divine grace and avoid the final judgment of God.[127] Luther's chain of reasoning, however, links self-accusation and justification together in a somewhat more complex pattern than mere antecedent and consequent: (1) the just man is the person who accuses and judges himself;[128] (2) the sinner, on the other hand, denies the Word of God which accuses him of sin and by rejecting that Word judges God to be a liar;[129] (3) the just man conforms his judgment to the Word of God and so justifies God in his judgment;[130] (4) though a sinner in fact, the just man becomes a sinner in his own estimate by acknowledging the truth of his situation before God;[131] (5) the sinner who justifies God justifies himself at the same time.[132] That is to say, he receives the justification which God grants to those who give up the struggle to establish their own righteousness and who risk everything on what appears to be the insubstantial promise of God.

While self-accusation seems at times to be the presupposition of the act of justifying God, at other times they are synonymous. In any case, the precondition for both self-accusation and the justification of God is the Word which condemns and justifies.[133] The content of self-accusation is not monastic asceticism, but conformity to the words and promises of God, which encounter the sinner as both letter and spirit, law and gospel. The sinner does not become morally worthy by self-accusation and the act of justifying God.[134] Rather he acknowledges for the first time the extent of his own unworthiness. God has promised to give his grace to those who admit the painful truth about themselves and who seek their salvation in God alone. The covenant with God is fulfilled, not by demonstrating one's virtue, but by acknowledging and bemoaning one's sin.

125. WA 4.192.26–30.
126. WA 3.288.30–32; 3.370.18.
127. WA 4.198.19–21.
128. WA 3.288.30–32; 55².33.1–4.
129. WA 3.288.8–12.
130. WA 55².24.6–12; 3.288.24–25.
131. WA 3.288.6–7.
132. WA 3.291.26–28.
133. Not only is the Church created by the Word of God (cf., for example, WA 4.189.17–25), but the faith and grace which justify the sinner rest on a *testamentum* or *pactum Dei* (WA 3.289.1–10).
134. WA 3.284.15–19.

Luther extends this idea in his contrast of judgment (*iudicium*) and righteousness (*iustitia*). *Iudicium* has three primary meanings for Luther. When the psalmists use the word, they may have reference to the judgment by which sinners are judged by God.[135] This judgment is imposed, willy-nilly, by God and is not necessarily hailed by the sinner who suffers it as a welcome discipline. *Iudicium* can also refer to self-accusation, the sentence of condemnation which one solemnly hands down against one's own sins. Judgment in this sense is the sinner's acknowledgment that he is indeed worthy of punishment and death.[136] But *iudicium* has a third primary meaning as well. It can designate the faith by which the Lord judges the righteous. In this understanding judgment is not something which we do but something which we suffer to be done to us as we conform our *iudicium* to the *iudicium Dei*.[137]

In addition to these three primary meanings, Luther sometimes uses *iudicium* as a synonym for the Word of God which is the bearer of his message of judgment and grace. The Psalmist actually has this meaning in mind when he protests that "I have not turned aside from your judgments." Since *iudicium* is a synonym for the Word of God, it can also serve as a designation for Jesus Christ, who is himself the Word and Judgment of the Father.[138] The Word of God is not simply a word of judgment as law or as letter, but even as a word of the gospel.[139] The gospel is a *iudicium* which separates the faithful from the faithless, the better from the worse, the children of light from the children of darkness. Indeed, it cuts more deeply and radically even than that, since the judgment of God in Scripture penetrates the inner life of man, dividing spirit from flesh. It cleaves the sinner in two and does not merely separate the just from the unjust.[140]

Luther contrasts the judgment of God with the judgment of men. The judgment of God unfailingly condemns the things which the judgment of men chooses and elects the very things which the judgment of men despises.[141] The perspectives *coram Deo* and *coram hominibus* are antithetical to each other. No more impressive evidence of this antithesis can be provided than the cross of Christ, where the strength of God is hidden by the contrary appearance of what men judge to be weakness.

The principal meaning of *iudicium* in the *Dictata super Psalterium* is self-accusation or confession of sin, that humiliation of the self in which

135. *WA* 55².20.21ff.
136. *WA* 55².20.21ff; 55².32.18–20.
137. *WA* 55².21.10–14; 3.291.9–21.
138. *WA* 3.466.4–7.

139. *WA* 55².107.20–24.
140. *WA* 3.368.3–5.
141. *WA* 3.463.15–18.

the sinner confesses his poverty and utter nothingness in the presence of God and conforms his trembling judgment to the severe mercy of the judgment of God. *Iudicium* is, quite frankly, humility, the admission that one is a sinner, unworthy of the least benefits of divine generosity and unable to reconstitute one's broken relationship with God.[142] Unless one is *in iudicio* in the sense that one has conformed one's judgment to the judgment of God by word and action, one is still in one's sins and not yet in the righteousness of God.[143] While Luther can speak as though this humility were the precondition for the reception of grace,[144] he can also confess that grace is granted simultaneously (*simul*) with the judgment of God.[145]

For the sake of his own name God dignifies the unworthy.[146] He reckons righteousness (*iustitia*) to those to whom he does not impute sin.[147] In granting righteousness God does not regard the merits or demerits of the sinner, but solely his own goodness.[148] Because God is Judge and not man, the sinner needs more than the public civility which will satisfy the lax requirements of his neighbors. He must have a righteousness which can satisfy the scrutiny of absolute Holiness.[149] And it is this kind of righteousness which God gives. He gives it because of his fidelity to his promises or, to use the language of the Psalms, because of his "truth." God has promised to justify the humble. When he acts in accordance with this promise, he is merciful for the sake of the sinner but truthful for his own sake.[150]

While the name of the Lord is great in itself, the act of justification makes that name great in us.[151] Luther cheerfully rings the changes on this theme. God is the righteousness with which we are righteous,[152] the strength with which we are strong,[153] the holiness with which we are holy.[154] God is called righteous and holy and virtuous,[155] not simply because he is that in himself, but, more importantly, because he becomes that in us. Holiness is ascribed to God because he communicates it to others.[156] The righteousness which God confers is valid *coram Deo* and

142. *WA* 3.208.33–34.   143. *WA* 3.203.6–12.
144. *WA* 4.91.4–5; 4.111.33–37. Cf. Steven E. Ozment, *Homo Spiritualis* (Leiden, 1969), pp. 182–83. See also *WA* 3.124.12–14.
145. *WA* 4.132.38–39; 4.133.12–14.   151. *WA* 3.523.33–35.
146. *WA* 55².55.4–7.   152. *WA* 3.451.17–19.
147. *WA* 3.175.9–11.   153. *WA* 4.275.15–17.
148. *WA* 3.351.33–38.   154. *WA* 55².75.9.
149. *WA* 3.283.36–39.   155. *WA* 4.231.5–9.
150. *WA* 4.13.29–35.   156. *WA* 3.127.8–13.

not merely *coram hominibus*.[157] It conforms in all particulars to the judgment of God.

Since God is just already, he does not need to be justified. Nevertheless, he *is* justified, if not in himself then in his words and in us.[158] God is justified when we rely on his faithful promise of grace for the humble. By conforming our judgment to his,[159] we are brought into conformity with One who can never be anything but true and just.[160] We are just precisely because we speak the truth. Confessing the truth makes us *conformis Deo*.[161] Christ dwells in those who dwell in the truth. It is an axiom of the spiritual life that "where truth is, there Christ is also found."[162]

Luther repeats the same themes over and over again as he defends the authenticity of the righteousness of God, even though it runs contrary to ordinary human expectation.[163] It is a righteousness of faith and therefore not one which is created by obedience to the moral demands of the law.[164] Luther defines it tropologically as faith in Christ (*fides Christi*).[165] Not only is it mediated through Christ,[166] but Christ alone forms the source and sphere for the justifying activity of God.[167]

When one asks how it is possible for faith alone to justify, Luther responds that it is not, strictly speaking, faith which does it. The testament or covenant of God (which rests in its own turn on the fidelity of God to his promises) provides the basis on which God justifies the sinner.[168] While Luther affirms that faith is the work of God which makes just men out of sinners[169] and that faith alone achieves this apart from works,[170] he also admits that faith is worthless apart from the truth of God.

Luther mentions the technical terms *fides informis*[171] and *fides formata*,[172] but he does not really use traditional scholastic categories with any frequency. Luther's emphasis lies elsewhere, on trust in the promise of God which contradicts what reason and common sense approve.[173]

157. WA 3.451.17–19.
158. WA 3.288.4–5; 3.284.21ff.; 3.292.27–32.
159. WA 3.291.9–21.   161. WA 3.289.31–35; cf. 3.291.9–21.
160. WA 3.289.31–35.   162. WA 55².34.2–4; cf. 3.285.5–7.
163. WA 3.111.10–12; 3.199.18; 3.451.8–10; 3.458.19–20.
164. WA 55².92.17–19; 3.179.2–5; 3.331.1–5; 4.248.1–3; 4.325.8–11.
165. WA 3.466.26–32; 3.463.1; 55².54.17–21.
166. WA 3.174.10–20; 4.2.21–22.   168. WA 3.289.1–10.
167. WA 3.155.17–23.   169. WA 3.532.13–16.
170. WA 4.271.29–33; 4.380.19ff.; 4.438.4–5.
171. WA 3.490.22–28.   172. WA 4.441.25–31.
173. WA 4.8.34–36; 3.228.11–18; 4.356.9–13; 4.95.1–4; 3.548.2–5; 3.141.23ff.; 3.548.6–9; 4.82.37–83; 4.83.3–9; 3.651.19–22.

Rather than talk at length about *fides formata*, Luther prefers to identify faith with wisdom (*sapientia*),[174] trust (*fiducia*),[175] or the substance (*substantia*)[176] on which one builds one's life. It is confidence in the promise of God concerning the "things which do not appear." It includes as a matter of course the two moments of self-accusation and confession of the praise of God. Wherever there is faith, there is conformity to the judgment of God.

This understanding of justification excludes the notion that one can be justified by the performance of the works of the law.[177] The proud, however, resist the judgment that they are sinners whose destiny rests in hands other than their own.[178] They attempt to establish their own justice which is nothing more than a poor parody of the real thing. But it suits them well enough and they are quick to take offense at the just souls who refuse to take part in their charade. By rejecting the righteousness of God, they demonstrate their true feelings about God. They deny that they are sinners and so make God out to be a liar;[179] they justify themselves in their own words[180] and so forfeit the only righteousness which matters, the righteousness of faith.[181] The righteousness of God excludes human righteousness,[182] always and without exception. That is a home truth which the proud, muttering and grumbling, exhaust themselves in a pointless attempt to deny.

In his marginal comments on the Sentences of Peter Lombard in 1509, Luther still regards love as the central principle of justification, though he rejects the notion that love is a habit and argues rather that it is the immediate presence of the Holy Spirit.[183] While faith orients the believer toward invisible realities, love is the crucial term in justification, the fundamental element on which all else depends. Faith justifies only in the sense that it is the faith which works by love.

Luther's emphasis shifts in the *Dictata* from love to faith alone as the principle of justification. This shift in the role of faith necessitates for Luther a corresponding shift in his analysis of its nature. While faith is still a complex action with several moments, the fact that it is no longer

---

174. *WA* 4.339.1.6.   175. *WA* 4.39.5–9.
176. *WA* 4.168.1; 3.649.17–20; 3.419.36–420.1; 3.410.16–19.
177. *WA* 55².92.17–19.   179. *WA* 3.170.33–34; 3.172.30–36.
178. *WA* 4.344.24–27.   180. *WA* 3.284.32–35.
181. *WA* 3.154.32–34; 3.172.2–6; 4.306.1–7.
182. *WA* 55².36.17–18; 3.154.32–34.
183. *WA* 9.90.32; 9.92.23; 9.90.27; 9.72.4; 9.72.11; 9.13.21; 9.47.6; 9.24.25; 9.74.10; 9.23.6; 9.27.22; 9.29.1; 9.42.31; 9.42.36; 9.42.39.

subordinate to love forces Luther to redefine its function in the process of justification. The character of this redefinition becomes apparent in Luther's reflections on the question of the proper disposition for the reception of grace.

At several points in his exposition of the meaning of justification Luther indicates that humility[184] or self-accusation[185] is the presupposition for the reception of grace. He qualifies that assertion, as we have seen, by affirming with equal force that the grace of God coincides with his judgment[186] and, to all intents and purposes, self-accusation and the act of justifying God are synonymous.[187] Nevertheless, it is true and cannot easily be denied that Luther also teaches that no one is justified by faith who does not first humbly confess his own unrighteousness.[188] Is humility, therefore, a virtuous disposition which is in some sense a cause of grace? Is Bizer correct when he stubbornly argues that the young Luther teaches justification by the monastic virtue of humility?

Fortunately, Luther has left extensive evidence on the question of the proper disposition for the reception of grace. Ever since the marginal notes on Peter Lombard and St. Augustine, Luther held that natural moral acts apart from the grace of God are not to be considered as genuinely good.[189] The goodness of a moral act is not separable from the gift of justifying love. That dogmatic conclusion does not deny the presence of *syntheresis* in the sinner.[190] But an inextinguishable longing for the Good and the ability to realize what is good in concrete moral activity are not the same thing at all.

Moreover, Luther teaches that God elects without any consideration of antecedent merit or foreseen use of grace.[191] While Luther does not emphasize the doctrine of election, he does agree with Staupitz in denying the nominalist position which equates predestination with foreknowledge of human merit. As election is conferred without consideration of the merit of the sinner, so, too, is prevenient grace.[192] Even if Luther had nothing else

184. WA 4.91.4–5; 4.111.33–37; 3.124.12–14.
185. WA 3.288.30–32; 3.370.18.
186. WA 4.132.38–39; 4.133.12–14; cf. 3.644.34–38.
187. WA 3.185.6–7; 3.284.37ff.
188. WA 3.345.29–30.
189. WA 9.71.6, 23, 32; 9.72.36. Cf. WA 4.18.25–29; 4.43.8–12; 4.211.10–12; 3.212. 4–7; 3.231.25–31; 4.207.22–7; 4.343.22–25.
190. WA 55². 113.4–5; 3.624.31–33; 4.255.21–24; 3.238.11–13.
191. WA 3.179.26ff.; 3.374.21–22; 4.422.21–22; 3.116.1–2; 3.116.25–26; 4.92.23–27; 4.81.20–22; 3.163.29ff.
192. WA 3.200.14–16.

to say on the subject of preparation for grace than this, it would be very difficult to sustain the thesis that humility is a virtue which merits the favor of God. Whatever else Luther may mean by asserting that humility is a precondition for the reception of grace, he cannot mean that.

Grace is not given to merits or even denied to demerits.[193] Indeed, the very intention to serve God is itself a gift of grace.[194] Against those theologians who wish to merit grace by the exercise of their natural moral powers, Luther tells a story of a prince who wanted to give one hundred florins to a subject as an expression of his favor. Nothing was required from the subject in return. Anyone can see, Luther argues, that a hundred florins as a gift from a prince is worth much more than the same amount earned as wages. The subject received more than money; he received the love of his prince.[195] Theologians who want to turn the relationship with God into an affair of wages and rewards have excised from it the most important thing, the love of God. The gospel is about gifts and love, not wages and rewards.

Luther attacks what he regards as a false understanding of preparation for grace. Some people, badly informed, think their own morally good acts have claim to the favor of God and are worthy of reward by God with justification.[196] But their viewpoint turns the gospel on its head. The proper understanding of preparation for grace is an issue with two sides. Primary in Luther's thought is the central role of the truth of God in his promises.[197] The real preparation for grace, apart from which all other preparation is utterly futile, is the preparation which God has made by establishing a covenant in which he promises to give his grace to real sinners. Real sinners are people who are sinners not merely in fact (all men are sinners in this sense), but who confess that they are sinners, who conform their judgment to the judgment of God and, by doing so, justify God in his Word of judgment and grace.

While primacy is given to the truth of God, to God's fidelity to his promises, as the fundamental and indispensable preparation for grace, there is a secondary ground in the sinner himself, far less important but no less essential. Luther does not believe that the sinner is capable of presenting a disposition of undisputed moral virtue as the basis of his acceptance by God. Even if he were capable of producing such a disposition apart from

193. *WA* 4.258.5–7; 4.258.30–33.
194. *WA* 4.309.10–11.
195. *WA* 3.192.2–5.

196. *WA* 4.17.10–17.
197. *WA* 4.38.37ff.; 4.17.17–26.

grace (and he clearly is not), it would be irrelevant as the ground for the justification of the sinner. In order to receive the strength and righteousness of God, the sinner must be weak and sinful. The whole have no need of a physician, only the sick and infirm. What the sinner offers to God in exchange for righteousness is his own sin. Not that his weakness and sinfulness justify him. Far from it! God alone justifies sinners, becoming their strength in weakness.[198] Nevertheless, it is human sin which has a claim on the pity of God.

The most famous passage on the subject of preparation for grace is the scholion on Psalm 113 [115:1]: "Not unto us, O Lord, not unto us, but to thy name give glory, for the sake of thy steadfast love and thy faithfulness!" In his exposition of this psalm, Luther compares the three advents of Jesus Christ—the advent in the flesh, by grace, and in glory—and draws several important theological conclusions on the basis of that comparison. Israel did not merit the incarnation.[199] Preparation was made for the first advent by a long genealogical descent from Abraham through David to Mary. But Israel's merits no more prompted the incarnation than its demerits could prevent it. God promised the messiah and it was appropriate for Israel, in response to that promise and in preparation for its fulfillment, to await expectantly the first coming of God in the flesh. And in the fullness of time, God did exhibit his Son to the faithful people who relied on the promises and covenants of God.[200]

This case has an exact parallel in the advent by grace. Luther illustrates his point by recalling once more the story of the prince and the hundred florins. This time, however, the beneficiary of the prince's generosity is no longer morally neutral. He is a robber and a murderer, a rogue and a scoundrel whose demerits richly deserve the gallows. Astonishingly, the prince pays no attention whatever to the moral failings of this man but makes him a wholly unexpected offer.[201] The prince will give the robber one hundred florins on the sole condition that the robber appear at a specified time and place to claim it. No terms could be more generous or less in conformity with ordinary human expectation.

Yet this story is a clue to the meaning of the gospel. The coming of Christ in grace is not a response to human merit but an expression of the simple mercy of a God who makes unusual promises and enters into gen-

198. *WA* 4.231.11–14.
199. *WA* 4.261.25–27.

200. *WA* 4.261.25–34.
201. *WA* 4.261.34–39.

erous contracts.[202] God offers his grace to real sinners. He will not be turned aside by the unpromising character of the objects of his generosity.

In what appears at first glance to be a sudden about face, Luther admits that those doctors who defend the thesis that "God infallibly gives his grace to the man who does what is in him" are in fact quite correct in their teaching.[203] But Luther does not invest this formula with the same meaning as Gabriel Biel, who believed that sinners could love God more than anything else in the world by concentrating their natural moral energies. Luther has spent too much time denying the premises on which that proposition is based for the proposition itself to have any appeal to him.

When one asks what Luther means by "doing what is in one," Luther responds with a string of verbs: "ask," "seek," "knock,"[204] "cry out."[205] The sinner does what is in him when he cries out for a virtue which he does not have and which he is all too painfully conscious that he lacks. The appropriate disposition for the advent of Christ by grace is a desperate cry for grace.

Prayer, of course, does not cause grace and only a fool would imagine that it merits it. The sinner like Lazarus stands with open hands before the gate of Dives. The criminal, to revert to Luther's own illustration, appears in response to the offer of the prince at the specified time and place. When Luther says that this disposition is *bene de congruo,* he is interpreting "the term *de congruo* as applying to the people's response, not to God's response to their efforts." Wicks is quite correct when in agreement with Grane and in opposition to Oberman he affirms that Luther's "agreement with nominalism is only verbal."[206]

The third advent in glory completes the parallel with the first two.[207] A holy life in the present is an appropriate disposition for those who await the third coming of Christ in glory. Christians who live "justly and soberly and piously"[208] in the present age do not merit the establishment of the reign of God in the age to come. A sanctified life is never fully worthy of the glory which will be revealed.[209] Nevertheless, acts of moral

202. *WA* 4.261.39–262.2.   204. *WA* 4.262.2–7.
203. *WA* 4.262.4–7.   205. *WA* 4.375.16–30.
206. Jared Wicks, *Man Yearning for Grace* (Washington: Corpus Books, 1968), p. 304. Cf. H. A. Oberman, "Facientibus quod in se est Deus non denegat gratiam: Robert Holcot and the Beginnings of Luther's Theology," *HTR* 55 (1962): 317–42; Leif Grane, *Contra Gabrielem* (Gyldendal, 1962); S. E. Ozment, *Homo Spiritualis*, pp. 162–83.
207. *WA* 4.262.7–17.   209. *WA* 4.262.8–11.
208. *WA* 4.262.7–8.

goodness are an appropriate expression of the proper disposition for the reception of the third advent in glory, just as prayer was an appropriate disposition for the second advent by grace. *Bene de congruo* refers to the disposition of the people of God, who conform their judgment to the judgment of God and await the disposition of all things at the last Great Assize.[210]

The sinner who is justified by grace alone without any regard to his merit or demerit is described by Luther as *iustus et peccator simul*. By this description Luther means to suggest that the Christian is "just" insofar as he already possesses the gifts and graces of God and "in darkness" to the extent that he still is imperfect and an object of the future generosity of God.[211] *Simul* characterizes the state of the Christian who has and does not have all that God offers him in the gospel. He has it in words and promises but not yet in fact.

If anyone still thinks that the *de congruo* disposition which Luther describes is a merit of congruity, Luther corrects that misapprehension in his scholion on Psalm 118 [119:41]: "Let thy steadfast love come to me, O Lord, thy salvation according to thy promise." The advent of Christ in grace does not come in response to the merit of sinners. There is, of course, a disposition which is appropriate to that advent, but it is a disposition which relies on the prior covenant of God rather than on one's own feverish moral activity.[212] According to the covenant of God, Christ is coming to sinners, whether or not he comes to me. But I pray that I may be included in his coming, that the second advent may happen in me. Does prayer, then, merit the second advent of Christ when virtue cannot? Luther would be willing to regard prayer as a meritorious cause if he could only find some justification for it in the Bible. But the Bible makes it perfectly clear that it is not *oratio* but *operatio* which is the principle of meritorious action.[213] Sinners can pray until they grow hoarse without earning a single merit of congruity. Begging that God will live up to the terms of his covenant is neither virtuous nor meritorious, according to the strict sense in which Luther uses the terms "virtue" and "merit," but it is the appropriate disposition for the reception of the second coming of Christ in grace.

While Luther denies that the proper disposition for the reception of grace is meritorious, he does not exclude entirely all consideration of merit from the Christian life. Although he attacks the opinion of Aristotle that

210. *WA* 4.262.11–17. 212. *WA* 4.329.26–36.
211. *WA* 4.251.10–17. 213. *WA* 4.390.22–24.

men are made just by the repetition of just deeds, he does not feel obliged to reject the traditional position that forgiven sinners are fortified by grace to perform works which are morally good and even meritorious.[214] Of course, all the goodness of their works is due to God alone.[215] The goodness of the Christian is never anything more than a derived goodness,[216] and would not exist at all apart from his faith in Christ.[217] In fact, Luther even goes so far as to maintain that the good works of the Christian are the works of Christ in and through him.[218]

In his exegetical comment on Psalm 118 [119:17], Luther describes the situation of the pious Jew in the Old Testament who merits a reward from God, not *de condigno* but *de congruo* on the basis of the promise of God.[219] Nevertheless, even though Luther is describing the situation of the pious Jew, he is uneasy with the term *meritum de congruo* and attempts to give a more Christian reading of the text. It is more Christian to think of the verb *retribue* as a word which refers, not to a reward for keeping the law according to the letter (*qui legem literaliter servabant*), but to the marvelous grace of God which renders good for evil, unlimited grace for actual guilt.[220] Luther has no objection to the idea that Christians are rewarded in heaven for good works completed in the power of grace, but he rejects altogether the notion of a natural morality prior to justification which God rewards *de congruo* with sanctifying grace.

Because Luther emphasizes the grace of God which is given by faith alone in Christ alone, he does not stress the role of human merits after the reception of justifying grace.[221] The principle is granted. Such merits do exist; they can be increased [222] and are rewarded.[223] Indeed, it is necessary to have our own merit in order to profit from the merits of the saints.[224] But Luther does not devote much time to this question because he has his mind on other issues.

Far more important to Luther is the fact that he now believes that justification is by faith alone rather than by love. It is a theme which he never tires of repeating. When more conservative theologians object that I Co-

---

214. *WA* 4.3.32–35; 4.18.29–36; 4.19.21–30; 4.113.14–17.
215. *WA* 3.283.6–9.
216. *WA* 4.115.25–26; 4.117.9–10; 4.211.1–4; 3.283.6–9.
217. *WA* 55¹.100.5–6.
218. *WA* 3.257.12–18; 3.545.30–35; 3.256.39–257.11.
219. *WA* 4.312.35–41; cf. 4.41.15–24.   220. *WA* 4.313.12–23.
221. *WA* 4.314.1–4; cf. 3.111.20–30; 3.404.22–24.
222. *WA* 3.126.20–22.   224. *WA* 4.239.14–16.
223. *WA* 3.111.20–30.

rinthians 13 teaches the subordination of faith to love, Luther responds that while it is true that faith passes away, the righteousness which comes from faith never does. In other words, faith is eternal because it grasps an eternal reality.[225] Therefore faith, while it passes away, is not subordinate to love, which does not. Luther admits the premise but denies the consequence.

About the life of faith Luther has relatively little to say. He quotes Sirach 2:1, a favorite passage with him throughout his life: "My son, if you come forward to serve the Lord, prepare yourself for temptation." [226] Temptation is the instrument by which God does his strange work of judgment in us in order to fit us for his proper work of mercy.

Temptations are a sign of God's favor.[227] They show us for what we are[228] and teach us humility, always an essential lesson for us to relearn.[229] By means of temptation God instructs us in a concentrated way in matters which we could never otherwise have hoped to understand.[230] Chief among those useful lessons is the increase of virtue[231] and joy in the Holy Spirit.[232]

While there are some temptations which one should fight, there are others from which one should simply flee.[233] Flight is not a sign of cowardice under such circumstances but a mark of wisdom. Temptation is not to be trifled with. No one is better able to describe the terrifying loss of powers which one suffers in temptation than is Luther.[234] Yet in spite of the dangers of temptation, Luther also knows (and it is a conviction confirmed by experience)[235] that the Word of God is efficacious against them. One can receive relief from *Anfechtung* by placing one's hope in the Lord.[236]

Luther has not entirely made up his mind in the *Dictata* what is the worst temptation. At times he identifies it with a kind of spiritual torpor and false certitude, which has lost the desire to be made better and so ceases even to be good.[237] At other times he identifies it with unfaith, the refusal to believe the promises of God, the disposition to subject every theological affirmation to radical doubt.[238] But perhaps the most profound

225. WA 4.249.29–30.
226. WA 3.376.31–32.
227. WA 3.340.13–14.
228. WA 3.146.12–14.
229. WA 3.109.35–39.
230. WA 55².55.19ff.
231. WA 55².58.2–5.
232. WA 55².58.12.
233. WA 55².58.12.
234. WA 3.168.25–31.
235. WA 4.232.1–5.
236. WA 3.169.6–12.
237. WA 55².64.4–6.
238. WA 3.578.38–39.

observation Luther makes on this subject is his comment on Psalm 68 [69]. There Luther contends that the worst temptation is to have no temptation at all, to sit in silence between the times bothered by neither God nor the devil. Not to be subject to God's strange work, however bitter, is to be deprived of the hope which his proper work creates in its place. "God is most angry," Luther warns, "when he is not angry at all."[239]

Luther does not devote much attention to resignation (*Gelassenheit*) or related issues. He does observe that the saints are more terrified by the prospect that they might blaspheme God than they are intimidated by the threat of the pains of hell.[240] While the saints are resigned to damnation if their damnation would serve God's glory, Luther hastens to add that the saints share an intense desire to avoid hell, since God is not praised there.[241] The conformity which interests Luther most of all in the *Dictata* is the conformity of the judgment of the sinner to the judgment of God, a conformity by which the sinner justifies God and consequently himself.[242]

Luther also repeats the theme he introduced in his marginal comments on Peter Lombard and Augustine that the Christian is one who is always beginning. Not to progress in the Christian life is to regress.[243] But one progresses in the life of faith, not by striking out in new directions, but by returning again and again to the first principles from which one starts.[244] God promises to give his grace to those who seek it. Therefore the Christian is someone who perpetually hungers and thirsts for righteousness.[245] He drinks the living water only to thrust out his empty cup again. On the last day of his life as on the first, he is justified by faith alone, not by faith and virtue.[246] No matter how much the Christian matures, he never outgrows the posture of prayer or the necessity of faith. Faith is the ground of the sinner's hope on his deathbed as well as at the moment of baptism.

III. *Conclusion*

The historian who traces Luther's doctrine of justification through 1500 pages of Latin text feels at the end rather dizzy, like a migrant laborer who has been asked to circle the same fruit tree several times a minute, picking

---

239. *WA* 3.420. 16–19.
240. *WA* 55².92.3–6.
241. *WA* 55².92.7–8.
242. *WA* 3.291.9–21; 3.289.31–35.

243. *WA* 3.110.2–3.
244. *WA* 55².64.12–14.
245. *WA* 55².64.20–25.
246. *WA* 4.350.11–16.

only one apple on each revolution. At the end of the day his baskets are full but his head is swimming.

Luther has no conscience about repeating the same themes over and over again, sometimes clearly, sometimes obscurely, frequently with a new twist or variation and just as frequently without. The development of his argument in the *Dictata* is anything but linear. It twists and turns, repeats and stutters, advances and falls back in confusion on itself. And yet in all this circularity, there is a unity of conception, a harmony between the dominant and subdominant motifs, which makes it new and vibrant and exciting. Luther may be repetitive, but he is rarely dull. And while his students may have left his classroom wondering what in heaven's name their professor was on about today, they never drifted aimlessly out with their minds a cipher.

Luther claimed as an old man that Staupitz had taught him to distrust his own natural moral powers and to hold to a doctrine of justification which starts with God's gifts to us rather than with our gifts to God. If one looks for evidence of these ideas in Luther's earliest writings, he will not be disappointed. The influence of Staupitz is very clearly to be seen.

Both Luther and Staupitz agree that humility is not a virtue prior to justification, since no human works prior to justification are really good. If humility is not a virtue, then by logical extension it cannot merit first grace, not even as a lesser merit of congruity. Virtue and merit are only possible in a state of grace.

While both Luther and Staupitz agree that the sinner should "do what is in him," their conception of "doing what is in one" bears no relationship whatever to the position of Gabriel Biel and the Tübingen nominalists. For Staupitz "doing what is in one" refers to the struggle of the sinner to avoid sin in cooperation with prevenient grace. The sinner attempts to bring his will into conformity with the will of God, invariably with pitiful results. He learns by bitter experience that the disinterested love of God and neighbor is an ideal goal forever beyond his grasp and so he throws himself without excuse on the mercy of God. In other words, the works of the sinner who does what is in him constitute in their mangled and mutilated form a prayer for grace.

For Luther "doing what is in one" changes meaning depending whether he has reference to the disposition appropriate to the advent of Christ in the flesh, by grace, or in glory. In the case of the advent of Christ by grace the appropriate disposition of the sinner is not to scurry about attempting to add to his store of natural virtues. Biel's image of the pilgrim as a noble figure who can exercise heroic virtues in a state of nature if he will only put his whole mind to it is a cruel illusion. Luther does not fire a polemical salvo against Biel's doctrine of justification but he dismisses it as irrelevant.

The proper disposition for justification is prayer. The sinner cries out for salvation, groans like Christian before he has opened the wicket gate, and awaits with eager expectancy on God, who is truthful and cannot lie, to make good on his promises. The verbs which give theological content to "doing what is in one" are "ask," "seek," "knock." Luther's sinners accuse themselves of sin and justify God in his judgment. It is by becoming a real sinner that Luther and Staupitz take advantage of the good news that the only thing we have to offer in exchange for grace—namely our ingrown and besetting sin—is exactly what God asks us to give him. The gospel is not "give me your virtue and I will crown it with grace" but "despise your sin and I will shower you with mercy." This stress on being a real sinner and on justifying God is an accent which one finds first in Staupitz and there is every reason to think that Luther took these themes over from him, they conform so admirably to the pastoral advice which Luther later recollects and reports.

But substantial agreement does not mean unanimity of opinion. The differences between Luther and Staupitz we noted in the preceding chapter over the role of faith and the place of election in the structure of their theologies as a whole remain to divide them when they talk of justification. For Staupitz justification is the execution in time of an eternal decree of God which is brought to fruition in the sinner by the gift of love. For Luther justification is trust and confidence in the promises of God which blatantly contradict the ordinary expectations of sane and sensible people. That difference is fundamental and qualifies the points on which they do agree.

Bizer is both right and wrong in his argument concerning the relationship of Luther and Staupitz during the crucial years 1513 to 1515. Luther and Staupitz agree over a great many issues touching the question of the justification of the sinner and in some of those agreements Luther has surely been influenced by Staupitz. But Bizer has not correctly understood the nature of those agreements.

When Luther and Staupitz taught that God gives his grace to the humble, they did not mean to imply that virtue is the ground on which justification occurs and the historian is mistaken who infers that from what they did say. When they speak of preparation for grace, they intend first of all to celebrate God's preparation in his election and covenants. When they allude to a proper disposition for the reception of grace, they have reference to the honest admission that the sinner is powerless to reconstitute his own broken and tangled relationship to God. And yet while they agree that humility is not a virtue, much less a merit, they do not understand humility in exactly the same way. For Staupitz the humble are the elect; for Luther they are the believers.

IV. THE MIND OF PAUL

In a remarkable passage in a letter which accompanies his Resolutions to Pope Leo X written in 1518 (*WA* 1.525.4ff.), Luther indicates that a word from Staupitz on the nature of true penance not only proved to be a decisive turning point in his own theological development but a hermeneutical key which clarified for him the biblical teaching on the subject of repentance. Twenty-seven years later in his Preface to his Latin Writings, in a passage which is almost a duplicate of his early confession, Luther argued that it was a sudden insight into what Paul meant by "righteousness" which revolutionized his thinking and unlocked for him the central message of the Bible. The question which naturally occurs to anyone who reads these two passages side by side is to what extent they are an exegetical comment on each other. Was Luther describing two different but equally crucial moments in his early development or is he distinguishing two aspects of one Copernican revolution? And if Staupitz was instrumental in assisting Luther to grasp the biblical meaning of penitence, can one assume that he was also instrumental in opening up for Luther the mind of Paul?

Both Luther and Staupitz were intensely preoccupied with the interpretation of Paul during the years 1515 to 1517. Luther lectured at Wittenberg on Romans (1515–16) and Galatians (1516–17), while Staupitz preached on several Pauline themes in Nuremberg through the Advent season of 1516. It would not, of course, be correct to leave the impression that Staupitz was concerned with Paul in his sermons to the exclusion of other biblical themes, notably motifs drawn from the Gospel of Mark. But it is the Pauline material, especially Romans 5–11, which lies at the heart of Staupitz's preaching. This wealth of Pauline exegesis makes it possible for us to examine the question whether Luther in his approach to the mind of Paul was influenced in any significant degree by the Pauline interpretation of John Staupitz.

In order to provide a larger framework for a comparison of the Pauline interpretation of Luther and Staupitz, we shall examine as well the Pauline exegesis of Wendelin Steinbach, who was Biel's successor at the University of Tübingen and the editor of his published works.[1] Steinbach was

1. For the relationship between Steinbach and Staupitz see H. A. Oberman, *Werden und Wertung der Reformation, Vom Wegestreit zum Glaubenskampf, Spätscholastik*

personally known to Staupitz and in fact delivered the principal address at the ceremony which promoted John Staupitz to the degree of Doctor of Theology. Luther, who was well read in Biel, knew Steinbach by name, though they never had occasion to meet. Steinbach lectured on Galatians at about the same time (1513) that Luther and Staupitz were struggling to understand the mind of Paul. The institutional ties between Tübingen and Wittenberg, the personal ties between Steinbach and Staupitz, and the theological ties between Steinbach and Luther justify the choice of Steinbach as an outside examiner on Paul.

There are certain themes common to the exegesis of all three men. Each comments at length on the Pauline doctrines of election and justification and worries about the hermeneutical problem posed by the Pauline theological vocabulary, a vocabulary which differs in some respects from the language currently in use in university faculties of divinity. These common themes offer us a convenient point of reference for assessing the influences at work on Luther prior to 1518. To what extent was Luther drawn backward to an image of Paul compatible with the principles of German nominalism? To what extent was he under the sway of Staupitz's understanding of the mind of Paul, a Paul refracted through Augustinian lenses? And to what extent did he pursue an independent course and sketch a new outline of Pauline thought, one which could not possibly be derived from the Pauline interpretation of John Staupitz?

1. The Image of Paul in the Theology of Wendelin Steinbach

During the last years of his life Wendelin Steinbach, who represented Occamist theology at Tübingen from 1486 to 1517, found his theological assumptions challenged to the hilt by his study of the epistles of Paul and by his wide reading in the Amerbach edition of the writings of Augustine.[2]

---

und Reformation II (Tübingen: J.C.B. Mohr, 1977), pp. 97–140. For the life and theology of Steinbach see Helmut Feld, Martin Luthers und Wendelin Steinbachs Vorlesungen über den Hebräerbrief, Veröffentlichungen des Instituts für Europäische Geschichte 62 (Wiesbaden, 1971); Die Anfänge der modernen biblischen Hermeneutik in der spätmittelalterlichen Theologie (Wiesbaden, 1977), pp. 70–83; "Die Hermeneutik Wendelin Steinbachs nach seinem Kommentar über den Galaterbrief," in Histoire de l'exégèse au XVIe siècle, Etudes de philologie et d'histoire 34, ed. Olivier Fatio (Geneva: Librairie Droz, 1978), pp. 300–311. For the critical edition of Steinbach's commentary on Galatians, see Helmut Feld, ed., Wendelini Steinbach, Opera Exegetica Quae Supersunt Omnia I (Wiesbaden, 1976). [Hereafter cited as Steinbach.]
    2. Melanchthon, who was resident in Tübingen from 1512 to 1518 while pursuing

Steinbach had been taught by his mentor, Gabriel Biel, that sinners could by the proper use of their natural moral endowments earn the first grace of justification by a merit of congruity.[3] Such a view came perilously close to the Pelagian views which Augustine had so roundly condemned. Not that Biel thought for one moment that his views were Pelagian! On the contrary, he was convinced that he had added all the proper Augustinian safeguards to his doctrine of grace to preserve it from any such charge.

Still the concentrated reading of massive doses of Augustine and Paul proved unsettling for Biel's erstwhile disciple, Steinbach, who was more accustomed to deal with Augustine as a series of vetted quotations in a manual of theology. But Paul and Augustine, taken in context and at face value, held positions which directly conflicted with several fundamental principles of Occamist thought. It was all very unnerving for Steinbach, who would have preferred to discover that all his favorite authors sweetly harmonized with one another. Instead, Steinbach found that his most important ancient authorities clashed dreadfully with his most esteemed modern ones.

The problem, however, was largely a hermeneutical one.[4] Steinbach was willing to concede (who, after all, could deny it?) that certain opinions of Paul and Augustine, if taken at face value, could not be harmonized with certain opinions of Biel. But then, too, not everything uttered by Paul pleased Augustine in its stark and unqualified form. And even the old Augustine found it necessary to go through his earlier writings with a blue pencil, adding footnotes and marginal notations. In short, theological language is historically conditioned. It is affected by the pastoral or polemical situation in which the theologian finds himself when he writes.[5] Ways of talking about God which are appropriate and useful in one historical epoch may prove misleading, even dangerous, in another.[6]

It is possible to take any number of examples of the historical character of theological language from the writings of Augustine.[7] For example, Augustine appears to deny that human moral activity can be virtuous

his studies, called Steinbach an "adsiduus lector . . . sacrorum librorum, et Augustini." See Feld, Hebräerbrief, p. 9.

3. On the theology of Biel see H. A. Oberman, The Harvest of Medieval Theology (Cambridge, Mass.: Harvard University Press, 1963), pp. 131ff. For additional bibliography on this subject see my article, "Late Medieval Nominalism and the Clerk's Tale," The Chaucer Review 12 (1977): 38–54, especially pp. 51–54.

4. Feld, Hebräerbrief, pp. 201–13; Oberman, Werden und Wertung, pp. 118–40.

5. Oberman, Werden und Wertung, p. 127.

6. Steinbach, III.17.136.1–7.   7. Steinbach, III.17.135.1–11.

or good *de genere* without the gift of infused love.[8] While Steinbach admits that infused charity belongs to the substance of the act of loving God and that good works should have a habitual relationship to God as their final end, he is not willing to deny free will or virtue to sinners who are still outside a state of grace.[9] If the literal sense of Augustine's proposition is true—no virtue without charity—then it is impossible for a sinner to earn justifying grace by a merit of congruity, a position Steinbach wants desperately to maintain. If one distinguishes, however, between Augustine's way of speaking and the real content of his theology, this tension is dissipated and Augustine can be shown to harmonize with the best Occamist theology.[10]

What is true of Augustine is also true of Paul.[11] When Paul asserts that Abraham was justified by his faith and implies that Abraham was justified by faith alone, he is putting forward a claim which any competent theologian knows is not true. James 2[12] as well as I Corinthians 3 and 13[13] demonstrates that the faith which justifies is a faith formed by love (*fides caritate formata*).[14] Steinbach is enough of an Occamist to believe that there is no inherent power in charity which by its own nature merits eternal beatitude. The law that a sinner must have a habit of grace is a regulation established freely by the ordained power of God. Love, therefore, has no necessary causality, but only a causality sine qua non.[15] Still it is infused love and not faith which is the real principle of justification.[16] What on earth could Paul have meant when he claimed that Abraham was reckoned as righteous by God on no other ground than his faith?

What we have here, in Steinbach's opinion, is a particularly outrageous example of Paul's peculiar *modus loquendi*. When Paul says that Abraham is justified by faith and implies by this that Abraham is justified by faith *alone,* he is using a way of talking appropriate for catechumens who are not yet fully aware that faith alone (in the sense of unformed or acquired faith) cannot save.[17] Only faith working by love saves. St. Paul knew

---

8. Steinbach, V.30.262.24–28.
9. Feld, *Hebräerbrief*, pp. 208–9.
10. Steinbach, III.17.135.15–21.
11. Steinbach, III.18.142.14–143.1.
12. Steinbach, III.16.131.11–18.
13. Steinbach, III.17.134.20–25.
14. Steinbach, III.17.136.22–137.2.
15. Steinbach, V.30.264.5–8.
16. Steinbach, III.16.131.11–18; III.17.134.20–25; III.17.136–137.2.
17. Steinbach, III.17.134.12–17. See Oberman, *Werden und Wertung,* p. 127: "Das 'sola fide' wird damit nicht, wie bei Biel und in der Tradition üblich, zurückgewiesen, sondern als *modus loquendi* des Apostles—und Augustins—durchaus akzeptiert, jedoch nur für den christlichen Anfänger, der noch nicht voll im Bilde ist, daß der Glaube allein Gott keinesfalls genügt."

that as well as St. James. What St. Paul is claiming (and we must be careful not to miss his point or be thrown off by his incautious phraseology) is that Abraham merited the first grace of justification by his good works, preeminently the good work of believing God with his unformed faith.[18]

In other words, the career of Abraham is an illustration of the theological principle which Biel cites with great regularity: "God does not deny his grace to those who do what is in them." Abraham did what was in him.[19] He was a virtuous man who struggled to love the God who had called him from Ur of the Chaldees and who grasped the promises of God with his own unformed and therefore imperfect faith. He performed works which were good *de genere* and by them merited the infused love which would form his faith and make it saving.[20]

If Paul meant only to suggest that Abraham merited grace by his unformed faith, why did he express himself in such a careless and exaggerated way in Romans 4 and Galatians 3? The answer for Steinbach lies in the mystery of divine providence. The excessive language of Paul (not excessive, of course, if one knows how to read it properly) concerning the faith of Abraham provided the later Pelagian heretics no foundation in Paul's letters to which they could rightfully appeal in support of their ideas.[21] The theological situation of the Church in the first four centuries dictated the kind of polemical rhetoric at which Paul was master.

Now, however, that the Pelagian heresy has been met and successfully weathered by the Church, the need for more restrained and precise theological language requires the Church to rephrase the moderate intentions of Paul in forms appropriate to their real meaning. Theologians *post Pelagium* can, without eroding the authority of either Paul or Augustine, use language and formulations which they themselves *ante Pelagium* would have rejected.[22]

When the text from Genesis which Paul quotes says that "Abraham believed God and it was reckoned to him for righteousness," it means that Abraham believed God with an unformed faith which earned the gift of infused love. He earned it, of course, *de congruo* and not *de condigno*, but merit it he did. Once having merited the gift of love, Abraham could be-

18. Steinbach, II.12.97.1–4; III.15.118.16–20; III.16.131.6–10; III.17.136.5–9; III.21.176.13–21. Cf. III.18.144.2–4; III.19.152.7–9.
19. Steinbach, III.16.129.26–130.6.
20. Steinbach, III.19.152.7–9; III.15.118.16–20; III.15.119.1–15.
21. Steinbach, III.17.132.19–133.1; III.17.136.1–7.
22. Oberman, *Werden und Wertung*, p. 134.

lieve God with a formed faith and be in the full sense of the term a righteous man. Indeed, one can find no better illustration of the nominalist view that sinners merit grace by their virtue than the Pauline image of Abraham.

Steinbach does not feel obliged to apply his hermeneutical distinction to Paul's doctrine of election, very probably because there is already a tradition of interpreting Paul on this question which Steinbach finds satisfying. Steinbach belongs to a school which identifies predestination with prescience. God elects to eternal life precisely those pilgrims who will merit grace by their own moral exertions and who will persevere in a state of grace (with due allowance for some brief lapses) until the day of their death. Their merit is foreknown by God and so serves as the basis of their election.

Other questions interest Steinbach more than the question of the legitimacy of the Occamist tradition which identifies predestination with prescience.[23] One such issue is the problem of the contingency of the future. To the double query whether revelation alters the contingency of the future[24] and whether the contingency of the future undercuts the doctrine of predestination,[25] Steinbach replies with an emphatic no. Neither the foreknowledge of God nor the revelation by God of things still to happen imposes any necessity whatever on the contingency of future events.

Or perhaps that should be stated more circumspectly. Human history is not subject to absolute necessity (*necessitas consequentis*), though it is subject to conditional necessity, the kind of necessity which holds that if A is granted, B must follow. This conditional necessity or *necessitas consequentiae* underlies the reliability of divine revelation and of the succession of contingent acts in history by which God redeems the world.[26] Human will is never subject to absolute necessity but it is caught up as actor and subject in a web of contingent events which follow from the decision of God to create and redeem.[27] What God has revealed will happen, not because the future has lost its contingent character but because it is governed by a contingent necessity grounded in divine immutability.[28]

23. Steinbach. IV.24.204.9–16. On this passage H. A. Oberman, *Werden und Wertung*, p. 128, comments: "Mit dem Begriff 'Erwählung' meint Steinbach allerdings etwas grundsätzlich anderes als Staupitz, denn es handelt sich nicht um die Vorherbestimmung, sondern um die Vorausschau Gottes, der vorhergesehen hat, wer das Gnadenangebot verwirklichen und wer abtrünnig werden wird."

24. Steinbach, I.4.29.5–10.
25. Steinbach, I.4.29.17–22.
26. Steinbach, I.4.34.17–20.

27. Steinbach, I.5.37.4–7.
28. Steinbach, I.6.51.25–26.

No one compelled God to create the world or save it in Christ. But by his eternal decisions God has set in motion a chain of events which take place by conditional necessity. The chain of events is itself guaranteed by the immutability of God. Steinbach is perfectly willing to say that the fruit of the Spirit is owed to the elect[29] and to use the verb *debere* to link the eternal election of God with the justification in time of a particular sinner. Granted the fact of election, justification takes place by contingent necessity. Of course, the force of that assertion is weakened somewhat by the admission that election is based on the prior foreknowledge of God, so that an eternal decision is qualified by a future contingent historical fact.

Not everyone who appears to be elect actually is. Steinbach draws a familiar distinction between people who are elect according to present justice (that is to say, they are currently in a state of grace) and people who are elect according to the intention of God (who may at the moment be in a state of sin).[30] People who are elect solely according to present justice will eventually fall into a state of mortal sin from which they will not be rescued and will die alienated from God and subject to eternal damnation.[31] Even though election is based on foreknowledge, it is not any the less essential for the eternal beatitude of the sinner.[32] Present justice divorced from the intention of God is not sufficient to save sinners.[33]

II. *The Pauline Interpretation of John Staupitz*

Staupitz seems serenely unaware of a need to reconcile the sharpest formulations of St. Paul with the formulations of scholastic theology. He is impressed, not with the discrepancy between contemporary theological language and the formulations of the ancient Church, but with the inadequacy of all language, ancient and modern, to capture the mystery of divine grace.[34] Staupitz is more concerned to avoid *curiositas vana*, an inclination to attempt to penetrate the divinely established boundaries for human reason and wrest an answer from eternal wisdom on questions to which no satisfying human answer is possible.[35]

29. Steinbach, V.33.285.18–22.   31. Steinbach, IV.24.204.11–16.
30. Steinbach, IV.24.202.23–30.
32. An old but still invaluable work on this subject is Paul Vignaux, *Justification et prédestination au XIVe siècle, Duns Scot, Pierre d'Auriole, Guillaume d'Occam, Grégoire de Rimini* (Paris, 1934).
33. On the question of present justice see H. A. Oberman, *Harvest*, pp. 217–20.
34. Staupitz, *Libellus* 23, 140.   35. Staupitz, *Libellus* 217.

True and substantial wisdom consists of the knowledge of God and of oneself. In achieving this wisdom human language is woefully inadequate for its task. This insufficiency of human language applies not only to the formulations of contemporary scholastic theology—of which Staupitz is skeptical—but even to the *modus loquendi apostoli*. To admit that inadequacy does not mean that Staupitz feels himself under any obligation to tone down the startling and abrasive formulations of St. Paul. Indeed, Staupitz sees it as his theological task to confront the Church of his own day with those formulations in their unqualified power and authority. But over all theological talk, whether modern or traditional, one needs to write a cautionary word. There is no way to talk about God without saying less than the mystery contains or more than revelation authorizes.

While Steinbach, who, after all, is commenting on Galatians, emphasizes what Paul has to say about justification, Staupitz is far more interested in Pauline teaching on election. And yet one is struck by certain similarities to Steinbach in the structure of Staupitz's argument. What is most striking is Staupitz's use of "conditional necessity" and of "debt."

According to Staupitz the central moment in the process by which a sinner is justified is the decree of election.[36] Election is not based on foreseen faith or on foreknowledge of the sinner's moral activity. Staupitz rejects absolutely Steinbach's doctrine of predestination. Election is grounded in a free and sovereign decision of God, uncoerced and finally inexplicable. But when Staupitz turns to a discussion of the historical effects of election, he uses the same categories as Steinbach: *necessitas consequentiae* and *debitum*.

The decree of election is immutable because it rests on the immutability of God.[37] All graces—justification, regeneration, glorification—flow from this initial and immutable decree[38] by conditional necessity.[39] Election makes Christ a debtor to the elect, so that justification is owed to them.[40] *Debitum*, *debitor*, and *debere* figure prominently in Staupitz's argument, just as they figure prominently in the argument of Steinbach.

But here the similarities end and the differences begin to multiply. Not only is election absolutely gratuitous but the causal relationship between election and justification is radically reconceived. Staupitz identifies predestination with first grace.[41] Election makes the sinner pleasing to God.

36. Staupitz, *Libellus* 218.
37. Staupitz, *Libellus* 86.
38. Staupitz, *Libellus* 27.

39. Staupitz, *Libellus* 22.
40. Staupitz, *Libellus* 26, 33, 34.
41. Staupitz, *Libellus* 21.

The love which is infused in justification, the so-called *gratia gratum faciens,* makes God pleasing to the sinner.[42] This redefinition of *gratia gratum faciens* represents not only a break with the theological tradition of Steinbach but with the tradition of medieval scholasticism generally. Indeed, it even represents a break with Staupitz's own earlier and more cautious formulations on this subject.

Nor can Staupitz agree with views of Steinbach on human freedom. Election is not only an expression of God's freedom, it is the sole guarantor of human freedom as well.[43] The freedom to do good works and so fulfill the ends for which one was created depends on election.[44] Without election there is no freedom, at least no freedom in the true sense of the word. The most one can claim for the human will apart from an infusion of grace is a certain spontaneity, but it is a spontaneity in the service of sin. Abraham (about whom Staupitz does not comment) is theologically significant because he is elect and not because he exercised his natural freedom to love God above everything else.

Staupitz does not shrink from the more controversial conclusions of his position. He is perfectly willing to admit that a distinction should be drawn between effectual and ineffectual calling[45] and that Christ died for the elect alone.[46] Such musings do not make Staupitz gloomy in the least. Indeed, he takes a good deal of comfort from the thought that salvation is utterly dependent on the mercy of a good God and is not endangered by the vagaries and instability of the human will.

This view of election forces Staupitz to address at some length the question of certitude of salvation. After conceding that no one knows whether he is elect apart from special revelation[47] and that the judgments of God are hidden,[48] Staupitz finds a number of grounds for reassurance. Suffering[49] and temptation are no obstacles to certitude, since God chastises those whom he loves[50] and even uses the sins of the elect to help them on their way.[51] Self-accusation and charity are also grounds for certitude,[52] especially in view of the fact that the reprobate are too insensitive to bemoan their sin and too self-centered to exercise charity. The sacraments as well should not be overlooked as assurances of grace, because they rest

42. Staupitz, *Libellus* 131.
43. Staupitz, *Libellus* 170, 172.
44. Staupitz, *Libellus* 45, 52.
45. Staupitz, *Libellus* 24.
46. Staupitz, *Libellus* 84.
47. Staupitz, *Libellus* 143.
48. Staupitz, *Libellus* 142.
49. Staupitz, *Libellus* 92.
50. Staupitz, *Libellus* 90.
51. Staupitz, *Libellus* 93.
52. Staupitz, *Libellus* 246.

on the trustworthy covenants of God with the Church.[53] Even mystical experience is a source of certitude for the elect.[54]

Parallelismus practicus (discerning the presence of grace from its moral effects in one's own disposition and behavior) is never rejected by Staupitz, though it is relegated to a secondary place as a lesser source of certitude.[55] Staupitz's Salzburg sermons of 1512 have already made it clear that the principal source of certitude for Staupitz is Christ crucified,[56] a theme echoed on the treatise on election when Staupitz affirms that anyone who has Christ has everything necessary for salvation.[57] Confidence centers in the cross rather than in endless self-analysis. While the certitude that one is elect is finally conjectural, there is ample room in that conjecture for tranquillity of conscience.

What sets off Staupitz's treatment of predestination in 1517 from his earlier reflections on it in his sermons on Job is not only his redefinition of *gratia gratum faciens* and his identification of election with first grace, but, more importantly, the rigor with which he grounds election in Christ. Christ is far more than the basis on which the elect are saved; he is the goal toward which they are directed. The elect are united to Christ in justification and conformed to Christ by a lengthy process of sanctification. Indeed, it is this very conformity to Christ which serves as one of the foundational props of the Christian's certitude. Whereas in his earlier writings Staupitz could claim there are no good works *de genere* apart from grace, he now insists that there are no good works outside Christ.[58] The decree of election is so intimately connected to the historical work of Christ in and for the faithful that it is impossible to talk about them in isolation from each other. To be elect at all is to be elect in Christ. Not even a formal distinction can be drawn between them, much less a real one.

Staupitz's reflections on justification are found both in his treatise on predestination and in his Nuremberg tabletalk, dating from the same period. The treatise on predestination focuses on the more general theological questions of justification and regeneration, while the tabletalk contains a series of unsystematic but nonetheless trenchant remarks on the sacrament of penance.

It is clear from the very first that Staupitz's understanding of the mind

53. Staupitz, *Libellus* 239, 240.   54. Staupitz, *Libellus* 62.
55. See in this connection my discussion of certitude of salvation in *Misericordia Dei*, SMRT 4 (Leiden, 1968), pp. 122–31.
56. Staupitz, Hs: bV8, St. Peter (1512), Sermo 12, fol. 58ʳ.
57. Staupitz, *Libellus* 237.   58. Staupitz, *Libellus* 19.

of Paul on justification clashes with Steinbach's. Since Staupitz identifies first grace with election, he places it outside the sphere where it can be merited either by the foreseen good use of reason or by foreseen good works.[59] Indeed, first grace is not even pursued by the sinner (*quam certe nemo petiit*),[60] who is lumpishly insensitive to the intensity of his predicament before God. This uncompromising statement of his position on preparation for grace not only represents a rupture with the more optimistic assessment of Steinbach but even contains an implicit criticism of his own earlier moderate use of "doing what is in one" in his sermons on Job.

Paul teaches that sinners are justified by faith.[61] Staupitz agrees with Steinbach that Paul did not mean to imply that sinners are justified by faith alone.[62] The Pauline doctrine is that sinners are made pleasing to God through election and then given the gift of love which makes their faith living and active.[63] Staupitz does not use the metaphysical langauge of act and habit to describe this love, preferring rather to stress the bond of charity as a personal union of Christ with the Christian.

Staupitz had employed the metaphor of a spiritual marriage to describe this union as long ago as his sermons on Job, but he now elaborates this theme with a thoroughness which makes his earlier observations seem rather pale by comparison.[64] The union between Christ and the Christian is so intimate that Staupitz even makes the startling claim that "Christ is I."[65] The union serves as the basis for an exchange of sin and righteousness. The Christian is just with a righteousness given him by Christ, while Christ becomes a sinner through his assumption of the guilt and weakness of the Christian. Staupitz does not regard this righteousness as something extrinsic to the sinner, something imputed to him.[66] The righteousness is intrinsic, something Christ effects in the Christian by his presence and activity.

While there are no good works *de genere* outside of this union with Christ, the elect, when they receive *gratia gratum faciens*, are prompted

59. Staupitz, *Libellus* 21.
60. Staupitz, *Libellus* 21.
61. Staupitz, *Libellus* 33; cf. 15.
62. Staupitz, *Libellus* 36.

63. Staupitz, *Libellus* 36, 152.
64. Staupitz, *Libellus* 54, 77.
65. Staupitz, *Libellus* 56.

66. A point also emphasized by Oberman, who observes: "Durch Staupitz' Fassung des 'Fröhlichen Wechsels' ist die Gerechtigkeit Christi nicht—wie dort—eine fremde Gerechtigkeit, iustitia aliena extra nos, sondern genau so wie die eigene Gerechtigkeit eine iustitia in nobis." *Werden und Wertung*, p. 112.

to do works which are both virtuous and meritorious.[67] Staupitz refuses, however, to allow the good works of the Christian to be regarded as merits of condignity, since only the works of Christ can claim to be merits in that sense.[68] There is too great a disproportion between the inherent worth of the moral activity of the Christian and the reward promised to such good deeds to permit anyone to think in terms of condign merit.[69] Besides, the good works of the Christian[70] are, in the last analysis, nothing more than the works of Christ in him.[71]

In the tabletalk the focus shifts from the doctrine of justification in general to the sacrament of penance in particular. Staupitz distinguishes between three kinds of penance. The first kind comes as no surprise. It is what the scholastics disparagingly called gallows' penance, a type of minimal attrition which regrets its sin only out of intense self-concern and fear of punishment.[72] Staupitz rejects this kind of repentance as utterly unworthy and wholly without any productive results in the reconciliation of the sinner with God.

One would expect the second and third categories to be, respectively, an active disposition of attrition and full contrition. Actually, they appear to be two kinds of contrition. Both are sorrow for sin springing from a love of God, but whereas the former is ineffective because it is not grounded in the sufferings of Christ,[73] the latter removes sins because it is.[74] By talking of effective and ineffective contrition—a curious and rather original way to talk—Staupitz rules out altogether attrition as a form of repentance. There is no true penance which is not firmly based in the love of God. The alternatives are either contrition or gallows' penance. *Tertium non datur.* The only question which matters is whether contrition is grounded in the sufferings of Christ.

That does not mean that the contrition of the Christian is perfect. Staupitz is simultaneously prepared to limit penance to contrition and to admit that human contrition is imperfect. God in some mysterious way never explained by Staupitz supplements the imperfect contrition of the sinner with the sufferings of Christ so that it becomes the kind of contrition it should be.[75] At any rate, it is obvious that the sinner whose contrition is

67. Staupitz, *Libellus* 19, 33, 52, 230.
68. Staupitz, *Libellus* 42, 51.
69. Staupitz, *Libellus* 37, 43.
70. Staupitz, *Libellus* 40.
71. Staupitz, *Libellus* 38.

72. Staupitz, *Rew*, Kn. p. 16.
73. Staupitz, *Rew*, Kn. p. 16.
74. Staupitz, *Rew*, Kn. pp. 16–17.
75. Staupitz, *Rew*, Kn. pp. 17, 19.

flawed should not be perturbed by his inability to repent as he should. God, who is easy to please and hard to satisfy, accepts even imperfect contrition when it is grounded in the sufferings of Christ.

Staupitz is very concerned to guard against the idea that repentance is a matter of external ceremonies and works of satisfaction. True repentance is always more internal than external.[76] Whatever the value of religious processions and pilgrimages, they cannot be allowed to take the place of a heart bruised by the sense of its own sin. Sodalities, confraternities, pious works, and charity are all important; far more important is internal grief over sin. One may be uncertain of the quality of one's repentance, but uncertainty may have a wholesome effect. If one is uncertain, one may repent all the more, confident that God sees the collection of the little penances and in mercy considers it sufficient.[77]

Staupitz lays such stress on internal contrition that he is even willing to admit that the sinner may be justified apart from the sacraments of the Church.[78] This is, of course, not a radically new position. Twelfth-century theologians such as Peter Abelard taught the same thing, to say nothing of the Tübingen theological tradition of Gabriel Biel. And like Biel, Staupitz makes the intention to confess to a priest part of the definition of true contrition.

Staupitz's conviction that genuine penance is internal and that external ceremonies are at best secondary leads him to severe strictures on indulgences. He does not deny that indulgences have a role to play, however limited, in the penitential process. But he presses home the point specified in the papal bulls that indulgences are not effective without penance.[79] Neither a papal bull nor the clank of guldens in the offering chest can free the sinner from the guilt and penalty of his sins.[80] Unless there is true repentance, an indulgence is utterly worthless.

All of which leads Staupitz back to a discussion of good works in which he more or less repeats what he has said in the *Libellus*. Justifying grace is the enactment in history of an eternal and hidden decree of God. No repentance is effective unless it is motivated by the electing grace of God. That is the sound old Pauline theology which the Church has always embraced when it is true to itself.

76. Staupitz, *Rew*, Kn. pp. 16–17, 19.
77. Staupitz, *Rew*, Kn. p. 18.
78. Staupitz, *Rew*, Kn. p. 17.

79. Staupitz, *Rew*, Kn. p. 18.
80. Staupitz, *Rew*, Kn. p. 18.

III. *Pauline Theology and the Young Luther*

Luther's reflections on the *modus loquendi apostoli* are far more radical than the views of Staupitz. Staupitz was only concerned to draw attention to the limits of all language, biblical as well as scholastic, for describing the mystery of God. What Luther seems resolved to oppose are the opinions of theologians like Steinbach who find in the distinction of the *modus loquendi apostoli* from the *modus loquendi noster* a way of reconciling the more inconvenient dogmatic positions of Paul with the more agreeable theological formulations of late scholasticism.[81] Steinbach was right, of course, to insist that Augustine did not defend exaggerated positions.[82] But Luther does not yield that point in order to trim Augustine's theology to the Procustean bed of German nominalist thought. Augustine did not indulge in theological exaggeration because his most abrasive theological formulations are true as they stand.

The language of St. Paul is implacably opposed to the metaphysical language of the scholastics.[83] In this clash it is the scholastics and not St. Paul who must radically alter their habits of speech. Paul's language is a challenge to a decadent and misleading way of pursuing the question of God, an approach at substantial variance from the biblical vision. The *modus loquendi apostoli* and the *modus loquendi scholasticorum* are antithetical. There is no hermeneutical device which can reconcile them. The sooner the Church admits that fact, the greater the likelihood of significant theological reform.

Luther has had very little to say about predestination until now. The correlation of faith and promise has been more important for Luther throughout his lectures on the Psalms than the relationship between the eternal decree of election and its implementation in history. But in his treatment of Paul, especially in his lectures on Romans, Luther addresses the question of predestination directly. It is obvious from his exegetical comments that his views do not coincide exactly with the views of Staupitz and are in sharp disagreement with the Tübingen theological tradition of Biel and Steinbach.

The agreements with Staupitz (and by extension disagreements with

---

81. *WA* 56.423.19–20; 446.11–16; 446.31–32; 447.19–27.
82. *WA* 1.224.7–8.   83. *WA* 56.334.14–18; 371.2–10.

Steinbach) are numerous. Luther does not accept the nominalist identification of predestination with prescience and does not believe that there is any way to remove the scandal or the mystery from election.[84] The corollary of such a stringent view of election—namely, that Christ died only for the elect—is embraced as readily by Luther as by Staupitz.[85] Heavy emphasis on predestination does not mean, of course, that sinners are saved by an eternal decree apart from its historical implementation. The elect are predestined to be saved by means.[86] There is no redemption for the elect apart from the actualization of the eternal decree in space and time. Election does not bypass history but rather guarantees the process of salvation within it.

There is even considerable agreement between Luther and Staupitz over the signs of election. Neither Luther nor Staupitz value self-scrutiny as a source of consolation. They direct the disturbed conscience away from itself and urge it to meditate rather on the wounds of Christ, the tangible and external evidence of the constant saving intention of God toward the penitent.[87] Security is a sign of the wrath of God.[88] There is no spiritual state more dangerous than the state of the man who suffers no temptation. The weak in faith should thank God for the temptations which terrify them and drive them to seek refuge in the crucified Christ.

Luther has other, more bracing advice for Christians who are strong in faith. They are urged to trust the naked mercy of God,[89] even to the extent of willing to be damned for the glory of God.[90] Real, hearty faith is always more concerned to glorify God than to secure its own salvation. *Resignatio ad infernum* (as this attitude was called) had been urged before on the spiritually mature and always in the knowledge that it is precisely the people who are willing to be damned who never will be.[91] Their very willingness disqualifies them. Hell is, after all, not a voluntary association.

But while there are impressive agreements between Luther and Staupitz against the Occamist tradition of Steinbach and Biel, there are disagreements as well, sometimes overt, sometimes implicit. The most obvious disagreement is over the usefulness of the distinction between absolute necessity (*necessitas consequentis*) and conditional necessity (*necessitas*

---

84. Against the doctrine of Biel that sinners can love God *super omnia* by the exercise of their natural powers, Luther asserts that man's willing and running is from God. WA 56.398.10–14.

85. WA 56.385.26–31.
86. WA 56.183.1–4.
87. WA 56.400.1–4.

88. WA 56.504.2–3.
89. WA 56.402.13–16.
90. WA 56.388.4–13.
91. WA 56.391.7–16.

consequentiae).[92] Steinbach and Staupitz find it a serviceable tool for explaining what they regard as the Pauline doctrine of election. Luther rejects it outright as empty sophistry.

While Luther's argument is fairly long and rather complicated, there are two points which lie at the heart of it: (a) if conditional necessity is applied to God, it implies a contingency in the divine will, which is patently false;[93] (b) if it is applied to the elect, it amounts to no more than an admission of their creatureliness, which is self-evident (one might even say, redundant).[94] On the other hand, Luther is perfectly willing to admit a "necessity of immutability" and offers the example that everyone is necessarily in sin (an immutable conclusion granted the fact of original sin) but no one is compelled to be (hence no necessity in the sense of involuntary compulsion).[95]

It is difficult to see how Luther's stress on the fidelity of God to his promises, a fidelity grounded in his own character,[96] is all that different from Staupitz's contention that justification proceeds by conditional necessity from the decree of election or how his own example of the necessity of immutability deviates in substance from conditional necessity when applied to the finite will of the creature. Luther is convinced that the distinction of *necessitas consequentiae* from *necessitas consequentis* is a theological dead end. But the structure of his argument remains, for all that, remarkably similar to the structure of the argument of Staupitz, who embraces the distinction without the slightest qualm. It seems, indeed, that the differences between Luther and Staupitz over this question are in the last analysis more apparent than real. By "truth" and "fidelity,"[97] to say nothing of the "necessity of immutability," Luther makes very much the same point as Staupitz with his more traditional philosophical vocabulary.

The real difference between Staupitz and Luther is not obvious at all, but it is the difference which matters. The difference, not to put too fine a point on it, is that predestination is a starting point for Staupitz, while it is not for Luther. The identification of first grace with predestination (a point Luther does not adopt), the redefinition of *gratia gratum faciens* as the grace which makes God pleasing to the sinner, the utilization of the distinction between conditional and absolute necessity, and the predilection for the terms *debere*, *debitor*, and *debitum* all have the effect of making

92. WA 56.382.16–383.24.
93. WA 56.382.21–27; 383.13–15.
94. WA 56.382.30–383.3.

95. WA 56.385.32–386.5
96. WA 56.210.9–13; 440.2–5.
97. WA 56.30.18.

predestination the first step in the historical drama of redemption. Once grant election and all the other steps in the *ordo salutis* will follow by conditional necessity.

Luther's approach is altogether different. He does not approach predestination like a kindly schoolmaster who is eager to show that if you will only grant him A, then steps B, C, and D will naturally, even necessarily, follow from it. Predestination is much more a wall of defence, an invisible circle drawn around something precious to protect it from harm. Luther's starting point is God's promise, a promise grasped by living faith. It is the correlation of Word and faith in their integrity and reality which is protected by the Pauline doctrine of election. The Word is only gracious and faith is only a gift if behind them lies the mystery of predestination.

No one ever accused Luther of being a systematic thinker or of showing concern with logical order at the expense of substance. But while Luther is not systematic in the sense that Melanchthon was, he is extraordinarily consistent in his approach to problems. A whole series of themes first developed in the lectures on the Psalms reappears in the lectures on Romans and Galatians. The tension between God hidden and revealed, between the theology of the cross and the theology of glory, between the strange and the proper work of God, between righteousness *coram Deo* and righteousness *coram hominibus* recurs in 1515 to 1517, whenever Luther addresses the question of justification by faith.[98] The reader who has grown accustomed to what Luther has to say about "truth" and "humility" and the "justification of God" will not be disappointed when he turns to Luther's exegesis of Paul. The correlation between Word and faith, so characteristic of Luther's interpretation of the Psalms, dominates his Pauline studies as well. By 1515 Luther knows that the sinner is justified by faith alone. What remains to be done is to work out the full implications of that very untraditional reading of St. Paul.

It would be tiresome to explain all these themes again and not really relevant. Not that Luther's treatment of them in Romans is boring—far from it! There is, if anything, greater clarity in the Romans commentary; the illustrations are more apt, the formulations more striking. But the central motifs are the same, however much Luther may play new variations on old themes. What needs to be done in this section is not to recapitulate

98. For a useful brief treatment of the central themes in Luther's lectures on Romans, see Gordon Rupp, *The Righteousness of God* (London: Hodder and Stoughton, 1953), pp. 158–91.

material already discussed elsewhere, but to single out themes in Romans, Galatians, and Hebrews—indeed, in all his writings of this period—which are new or which represent, to a greater or lesser degree, a significant change of direction. Not every change or development is worth noting, but some certainly are.

The first change worth mentioning is the fierce polemic Luther directs against the nominalist understanding of preparation for grace. Luther had already developed in his lectures on the Psalms an understanding of justification which clashed in principle with the views of Biel and Steinbach. But just as Luther commended the writings of Tauler long after he had developed an understanding of nature and grace which was very un-Taulerian, so Luther broke in theory with nominalist positions before he felt moved to attack them savagely. Perhaps Luther himself did not realize at the time that he was lecturing on the Psalms just how sharply he had broken with German nominalism. But there is no hesitation in his mind on this question when he turns to an exegesis of Paul. One can either embrace the Pauline doctrine of justification by faith alone or the nominalist doctrine. It is not possible to embrace both.

Some of Luther's polemic is directed against a wider front of late scholasticism than the territory occupied by Biel and Steinbach. When Luther attacks the Christian use of Aristotle (who holds, among other positions contradictory to St. Paul, that a person is made just by the repetition of good deeds) [99] or when he rejects absolutely as meaningless sophistry the scholastic distinction between conditional and absolute necessity,[100] he is striking at the positions of men who are themselves vocal, if not vociferous, opponents of Pelagian theories of grace. When he agrees with Staupitz against Steinbach that no works are good *de genere* without justifying grace,[101] he is even setting himself apart from Thomas Aquinas, who does not feel that a sound anti-Pelagian position commits him to adopt such an extreme Augustinian view.

But no matter how many swipes Luther may take in his lectures at Thomists and Scotists, his principal opponents are disciples of Ockham. He attacks with real gusto the nominalist use of *syntheresis*, their under-

---

99. WA 56.172.8–15; 349.23–26. Though Luther himself can cheerily use an analogy drawn from Aristotle in order to characterize five degrees in the Spirit. Cf. WA 56.441.23–442.5.

100. This point, already discussed earlier in this chapter in the context of Romans, is repeated in the *Disputatio contra scholasticam theologiam* (1517). Cf. WA 1.225. 33–34.

101. WA 1.224.13–14; 224.17–19; 225. 1–2.

standing of "doing what is in one," and their indefensible distinction between fulfillment of the law according to the substance of the deed and according to the intention of the law-giver.

In an early sermon Luther calls *syntheresis* a residuum of health in the
sinner[102] and affirms that nature can be revived through grace.[103] But
even in this early and, on the whole, positive utterance, Luther adds
qualifications which severely restrict the scope and competence of *syntheresis*. While *syntheresis* conforms to the will of God and always longs
for what is morally good and true, the blindness of reason and the deformity of the fallen will prevent the sinner from achieving the good for
which he yearns.[104] The question for Luther in this sermon as for St.
Paul in the opening chapter of Romans is not what one still knows of
the will of God but what one does with what one knows.

The deformity of human reason and will keep the sinner from doing
what he knows he should. *Syntheresis*, so far from providing a starting
point for the conversion of the sinner to God, manages only to increase the
responsibility of the sinner before God and consequently to increase his
guilt. It is difficult to see very much real difference, apart from terminology, between what Luther has to say about *syntheresis* in his early
theology and what Calvin has to say about *sensus divinitatis* in his mature
thought. Man knows and longs for what he cannot achieve; that is his
predicament. If he had no longing, he would not be human. But the question which matters is not whether the sinner has an impression of what
is good and a longing for what is better, but whether he can realize in
action the object of his longing. And for Luther the answer to this question is clearly no.

Luther presses his point further by insisting that only when the in-
carnate Word and Holy Spirit cleanse reason and will can they understand and love what *syntheresis* says they ought to love and do.[105] The
mere presence of *syntheresis* in Luther's first sermons and lectures is no
more an invitation to Pelagianism than is the presence of *sensus divinitatis* in the *Institutes* of John Calvin. To know and prefer what one cannot

102. *WA* 1.37.3–18; 32.1–8; cf. 36.11–19. For a discussion of *syntheresis* in Luther
which comes to essentially the same position as I do, see the very interesting book by
Michael G. Baylor, *Action and Person, Conscience in Late Scholasticism and the
Young Luther*, SMRT 20 (Leiden: E. J. Brill, 1977), especially pages 157–208.

103. *WA* 1.32.14–16.   104. *WA* 1.36.11–19.

105. *WA* 1.36.37–37.3. In 1512 Luther asserts that it is the will of God and not our
seeking, asking, and knocking which brings the new birth, *WA* 1.10.28–33. By 1517
Luther stresses the indisposition of the sinner to receive grace. Cf. *WA* 1.225.29–30.

achieve provides no foothold whatever for works-righteousness. *Syntheresis* without grace increases responsibility before God. Luther makes the point because he believes, quite rightly as it happens, that Paul makes the point first.

The problem with the nominalists is not that they posit the existence of *syntheresis*, but that they drastically overestimate its capabilities.[106] The will is weakly inclined toward the good. Luther in 1515–16 is still quite happy to concede that point.[107] But he digs in his heels at the suggestion that this weak inclination toward the good is sufficiently powerful to enable the sinner to love God supremely by the exercise of his natural moral endowments. It is ludicrous (Luther calls it a dream)[108] to compare this faint stirring of longing and desire with the wholehearted fulfillment of the first commandment.

All of which leads Luther to reject the astonishing claim of the nominalists that sinners can earn first grace by "doing what is in them." Sinners cannot love God more than they love any other creature, given the fact of original sin.[109] Nor is Luther willing to accept the distinction between fulfilling the law according to the substance of the act (by conforming one's will and actions to the moral law) and fulfilling it according to the intention of the law-giver (by possessing a habit of grace).[110] This distinction made it possible for German nominalists to explain how one could keep all ten commandments without the assistance of grace and still be saved by grace alone.

According to Biel no grace was needed to fulfill the law so far as the substance of the deed was concerned. God has made no law which fallen man cannot obey. But God has decreed that the just must have a habit of grace and that only works performed in cooperation with such a habit are full merits. By "doing what is in one," i.e., by fulfilling the law according to the substance of the deed, the sinner earns justifying grace *de congruo* and so is able to fulfill the law according to the intention of the lawgiver.

Luther rejects this theology with a howl of rage as a cloddish reconstruction of the gospel by "pig-theologians."[111] No one can do what the nominalists claim. Unless there is grace the sinner cannot love God at all, much less *super omnia*. To do what is in one without the help of God

106. *WA* 56.275.19–22.
107. *WA* 56.177.11–15.
108. *WA* 56.275.19–22.

109. *WA* 56.385.13–16.
110. *WA* 56.274.11–15.
111. *WA* 56.274.11–15.

is to commit mortal sin.[112] There is no acceptation of the sinner or of the sinner's works without the prior special assistance of God.[113] The distinction between "substance of the deed" and "intention of the law-giver" transforms the gospel into a second law.[114] Anyone who holds this distinction may not be a Pelagian in name, but he is a Pelagian in fact.[115] And so Luther rejects the nominalist doctrine of grace part and parcel as an unfortunate contemporary manifestation of an ancient discredited heresy.[116]

The position Luther took earlier in his commentary on the Psalms and which Staupitz has consistently maintained—namely, that the real preparation for grace is predestination—is repeated by Luther in his *Disputation against Scholastic Theology* (1517).[117] That does not mean that Luther denies it is possible for the sinner to do (in the language of the New Testament) "works meet for repentance." But these works—seeking, asking, knocking[118]—are impossible without the prior influence of grace and, in any event, do not cause the grace for which they prepare.[119] One can prepare for grace by works; one cannot obtain grace by them.[120] The sinner is indisposed to receive grace[121] until humbled by the Word of God.[122] Preparation for grace is primarily a matter of election and the preaching of the Word. Works prior to justification, never possible without grace and never good without justification, constitute a prayer for salvation but are not causative, not even in the sense of *causae sine qua non*.

Luther does not spend much time on the figure of Abraham in his early lectures on Paul, not as much as Steinbach does and not even as much time as Paul's discussion of Abraham could easily justify. But what Luther does say about Abraham is enough to reveal his fundamental disagreement with Steinbach's interpretation. Steinbach regards Abraham as the archetypal *viator* who earned his justification by "doing what was in

---

112. *WA* 56.355.19–26; Cf. *WA* 1.148.14–15.
113. *WA* 56.255.15–19; cf. 172.8–15; 248.25–33; 268.1–6.
114. *WA* 56.274.11–15.   115. *WA* 56.502.14–24.
116. When Luther stresses, as he does, for example, in a sermon preached in 1514, that good works are sins when they are not done in the fear of God, he is doing more than making the same point as Staupitz; namely, that there are no good works *de genere* without grace. Sin is for Luther not simply a moral category; unbelief or pride can be posited through morally good works as well as or even better than through works which are morally deficient. Cf. *WA* 1.38.2–5.

117. *WA* 1.225.27–28.   120. *WA* 1.118.16–21.
118. *WA* 1.10.28–33.   121. *WA* 1.225.29–30.
119. *WA* 1.147.10–12.   122. *WA* 1.201.10–21.

him." Abraham was not justified by faith alone, but by the faith which works by love.

Luther, however, who believes that justification is by naked trust in the fragile, apparently contradictory and unsubstantiated promises of God, regards Abraham as an example of an "absolute believer." By "absolute believer" Luther has reference more to the scope of Abraham's faith than to its constancy. Abraham is justified, not because he believes this or that promise of God, but because he stands ready to believe *any* promise of God, no matter how violently it may contradict the judgments of his own prudential reason and common sense.[123] Abraham's faith is not so much an act (e.g., believing Sarah will become pregnant in spite of her advanced years) as a disposition (e.g., believing that whatever God promises, however startling, he is able to perform). Steinbach's translation of Abraham's faith into pious works is, on Luther's principles, a fundamental misreading of Paul.

Luther's doctrine of justification by faith alone is enriched by his developing conception of human sin. Luther has already put himself on the side of Augustinians like Staupitz by denying the possibility of good works apart from grace and by stressing the weakness and instability of the human will, not only before justification (when one might reasonably expect to find it in a weak and debilitated condition) but even after baptism and the sacrament of penance.[124] Now in his lectures on Romans Luther introduces alterations in his doctrine of sin which cannot strictly be called Augustinian (though they are built on an Augustinian foundation). These alterations are stimulated by his close reading of St. Paul.

Luther is particularly impressed by the anthropological terms in Paul. Flesh and spirit are not higher and lower faculties in human nature; they are descriptions of the whole person considered in its different relationships. Flesh is not the body, but the whole person turned in upon itself in its irrepressible egoism and its radical alienation from God.[125] Spirit is the whole person in its openness to God and its trust in God's promises. Justification, as it touches flesh and spirit, touches the whole person. The

123. *WA* 56.267.9–12.
124. Luther repeats these themes in his lectures on Romans in such places as *WA* 56.274.8–11, 275.11–16, and 350.1–9. He rejects vehemently the position he held in 1509 that original sin is a privation of original justice (*WA* 56.312.2ff.). Luther describes the sinner as *homo incurvatus in se* (*WA* 56.356.4–6), a phrase which underlines Luther's holistic conception of sin.
125. *WA* 56.342.33–343.2; 356.4–6.

whole person trusts the saving promises of God (spirit) and yet the whole person remains a sinner (flesh) so far as the defects in its character are concerned.[126]

When Luther casts about for an analogy to explain how one individual can be simultaneously two persons, flesh and spirit,[127] he seizes on an analogy drawn from the ancient Christological formulations of Chalcedon. Just as Jesus Christ was fully human and fully divine, while remaining one person, so the believer is flesh and spirit, wholly sinner and wholly just, while remaining one individual center of moral responsibility before God.[128]

The believer is a sinner if one measures him by the absolute standard of the law of God. While justification brings a change in the moral character of the Christian, it never means that he is perfectly conformed to the will of God in all he thinks, wills, imagines, dreams, regrets. Sin remains a fact of human experience even in the believer,[129] though, paradoxically, the fact that one is a sinner is not known by a process of induction.[130] That can only be known by faith, as the sinner trusts the law of God which denounces his sin. If one attempts to determine one's status in the presence of God by an empirical sifting of the evidence, by an honest examination of conscience and rigorous self-scrutiny, one enters a labyrinth from which one cannot always escape, a maze in which the evidence is ambiguous and the possibilities of self-deception are endless. As odd as it may sound at first, faith is as necessary to Luther for the knowledge of oneself as a sinner as it is for the knowledge of oneself as a saint.

While remaining a sinner in fact (*in re*), the Christian is made just in hope (*in spe*)[131] and can therefore be described accurately as *iustus et peccator simul*, still flawed in his moral character and yet righteous in the judgment of God.[132] One has to be very careful not to misread Luther at this point. It would be easy to conclude that the contrast of righteousness "in hope" with sinfulness "in fact" is based entirely on an analytical proleptic judgment. In other words, God, who can afford to take the long view of matters, is prepared to deal with the imperfect present in the light of a perfect future. He reckons the believer righteous in the present because he will be righteous in the future.

126. *WA* 56.351.23–352.7; cf. 350.27–351.1.
127. *WA* 56.350.27–351.1.
128. *WA* 56.343.16–23.
129. *WA* 56.274.8–11; 275.11–16; 350.1–9.

130. *WA* 56.229.7–15.
131. *WA* 56.269.27–30; 272.17–21.
132. *WA* 56.270.9–11; 343.16–23.

That conception does not do justice to what Luther has in mind. Already from what Luther has had to say about hope in his lectures on the Psalms, one can assume that the phrase "just in hope" was designed by Luther to emphasize the point that the righteousness of the Christian is hidden from sight. If so, then the motto, "at once just and a sinner," implies both (a) that the righteousness which the Christian possesses by faith is hidden in the present under the contradiction and contrary appearance of his own sin and (b) that the promise which offers perfect freedom from sin touches a future still invisible to sight. Hope is contrasted with visibility. The righteousness of the Christian is not something which can be seen or empirically verified.[133]

What Luther is not out to do is to make future freedom from sin the basis of God's acceptance of the sinner. The Pauline teaching is that one is justified by faith alone, not by faith and sanctity, even if one grants that the future inherent righteousness of the Christian is a gift rather than an achievement. Already in the Romans commentary Luther is clear in his own mind that the believer is reckoned righteous in the present because of an alien righteousness. United to Christ by faith, he possesses a righteousness which belongs to him only by virtue of the *reputatio Dei.*[134] It is Christ and not the future contingent sanctity of the Christian that provides the basis for God's favorable judgment, his acceptance of believers in spite of their continuing unacceptability.[135]

Justification is a term which embraces the whole life of the believer. On the last day of his life as on every day preceding it, the Christian is justified by faith alone. Sanctity is never the basis for God's acceptance and approval, not even in the most minimal and restricted sense. No Christian existence is possible save on the ground of faith alone.

Obviously, Luther could not hold such views on the Pauline doctrine of justification without being forced, sooner or later, to reconsider what he had been taught in the late medieval schools concerning the sacrament of penance. In 1517 and 1518 while lecturing on Galatians and Hebrews, Luther began to outline what his new views on justification would mean when applied to the sacramental life of the Church. The occasion which prompted Luther's most acerbic and polemical utterances was the controversy over indulgences.

133. *WA* 56.58.15; cf. 50.16; 173.24; 174.2.
134. *WA* 56.22.25; 38.8; 158.10–14; 268.27–30; 269.1–4; 287.16–24.
135. *WA* 56.279.22–28.

Jesus Christ announced the imminent coming of the Kingdom of God and invited his listeners to repent. What exactly, Luther asked, did he have in mind?[136] Did he mean to urge submission to the sacrament of penance with its "cold works of satisfaction and its extraordinarily tedious act of confession"?[137] The Latin text of the New Testament with its translations of Jesus' words as "do penance" (*penitentiam agite*) certainly could give that impression. Underneath the Latin formula of the Vulgate, however, was the original Greek verb with its Aramaic and Hebrew antecedents. What was demanded by the preaching of Jesus was a "conversion," " a return," a "change of mind or intention," a fundamental turning of one's life to God, which begins but does not end with the first assent of the will to the gospel.[138]

The repentance to which a Christian is called is a continuous and lifelong process.[139] While conversion begins, as everything in history does, at some point in time, the process of conversion is not completed until every aspect of the human personality is driven out into the light of God's severe mercy, judged and renewed. Repentance proceeds layer by layer, relationship by relationship, here a little, there a little, until the whole personality and not merely one side of it has been recreated by God. Penance refers not only to the initial moment of faith, no matter how dramatic or revolutionary it may seem, but to the whole life of the believer and the network of relationships in which that life is entangled.

Luther agrees with Staupitz that true penance begins with the love of justice.[140] He is convinced that only those who love God can hate sin.[141] A thoroughly unconverted sinner is a perfect child in his knowledge of sin. Only a saint knows what sin is; and therefore only a person who has progressed in the love of God can see with sufficient clarity what exactly is the character of the sin which is distorting his life. It requires some growth in grace to repent properly. The more one grows in the love of God, the more perfect one's repentance. A new penitent, waiting to be admitted to the confessional for the first time, has, unfortunately, only a child's eye view of his own sin. Real repentance, real conversion of life is an activity of the spiritually mature.

Luther like Steinbach and Staupitz is a contritionist. Real penitence is

136. WA 1.233.10–13.
137. WA 1.526.10–14.
138. WA 1.525.24–30; 526.1–9.

139. WA 1.322.12–13.
140. WA 1.319.27–31.
141. WA 1.320.26–37.

concerned with offenses against God rather than with self-concern and anxiety about one's status in the presence of God.[142] Luther denies, however, Steinbach's contention that love for God in contrition is the product of natural moral energy unaided by grace. If that were true, then love of justice would be the last step in a process dominated by the exercise of human free will. But it is not true. The sinner loves God because God first loved him and demonstrated the extent and depth of that love in the wounds of Christ.[143] God's love, God's grace, awakens in the sinner the love for God which is always at the heart of true contrition. There is no true contrition and hence no true repentance outside Christ.[144]

Luther does not advocate justification by contrition. Steinbach's theory of justification falls flat on its face precisely because one can never be certain that one's contrition is perfect.[145] And unless one loves God *super omnia* without any qualification whatever, any hedging or fiddling, one cannot on Steinbach's principles be justified. But one should no more put one's faith in one's contrition than in one's good works.[146] The proper object for faith is the promise of God which offers salvation to everyone who places his sole confidence in Christ.[147]

If justification is by faith alone,[148] then the obvious conclusion to be drawn is that it is the faith of the sacrament rather than the sacrament of penance in the strict sense which justifies.[149] All talk about contrition and "not placing an obstacle to grace"[150] depends on the medieval tradition that penance as a sacrament of the New Law confers grace on the basis of the proper performance of the rite. Deny that the sacrament justifies *ex opere operato* and all theories of attrition and "obstacles to grace" collapse with it. Faith justifies,[151] not the sacrament,[152] not contrition,[153] not confession. Sacraments are not efficacious signs of grace merely because they "happen" (*fit*), as Augustine would lead one to believe, but because of the faith which is attached to the Word of God hidden in those visible signs.[154] The priest is important and plays a necessary role as an administrator of the Word of God rather than as a dispenser of sacraments which are effi-

142. *WA* 57.82.14–17.
143. *WA* 1.576.10–19.
144. *WA* 57.226.1–6.
145. *WA* 1.66.17–22; 322.16–19.
146. *WA* 1.322.9–10.
147. *WA* 56.45.15.
148. *WA* 1.544.7–8.

149. *WA* 1.631.7–8.
150. *WA* 1.632.33–35; cf. 324.8–19.
151. *WA* 57.170.1–10; 1.286.15–19.
152. *WA* 1.631.7–8; 57.206.2–5.
153. *WA* 1.596.7–9.
154. *WA* 1.594.40–595.7.

cacious in themselves.[155] Luther sums up his position in an aphorism: "Not the sacrament of faith but the faith of the sacrament justifies." [156]

Such a radical doctrine of penance has hardly left any space for even a minimal role for indulgences. A genuinely penitent, thoroughly contrite person wants to be punished,[157] or, at the very least, wants to make amends for the harm he has done.[158] An indulgence is a way of escaping the consequences of one's acts.[159] A sinner whose eyes are darting to and fro to find an exit when there is a real danger of being called to render an account for the conduct of his life is not someone who is truly contrite. The new disposition called for in the proclamation of Jesus is antithetical to the disposition which hawks and hoards indulgences.

Luther cannot talk about penance without returning to his old theme of real sin, real damnation in contrast to the game of striking pious attitudes played by "feigned sinners."[160] God promises to give his grace to "real sinners." "Real sinners" are people who conform their judgment of themselves to the judgment of God over them and so justify God in his words. Paradoxically, it is the real sinner who is justified by God and who knows both theoretically and experientially what repentance offers and demands.

The gospel as Luther conceives it is both easier and harder than the gospel Steinbach offered. Being a real sinner is a condition which, on the face of it, anyone can meet; but it is harder because it demands rigorous honesty in the face of the truth. The penitent cannot prepare himself for grace because he must be crucified by God's word of judgment and die. Repentance has to do with death and life and not merely with the decision of an already good man like Steinbach to improve his frankly unimpeachable character.

Luther's objection to Steinbach's theory is not merely that it harbors a thoroughly unrealistic view of human nature, though that is part of his objection. Even more important for Luther than the fact that no one can live up to Steinbach's theory of repentance is the fact that no one is expected to. The gospel does not demand moral virtue as the preparatory stage of penitence. Steinbach's view of the matter is not only unworkable; it is irrelevant. The sole precondition for authentic repentance is real sin; the sole preparation which matters is the preparation which God has made in the gospel.

155. WA 1.632.15–18; cf. 604.35–39.   158. WA 1.526.24–27.
156. WA 1.631.7–8.   159. WA 1.98.37–99.8.
157. WA 1.235.16–17.   160. WA 1.184.22–26; 370.9–13.

IV. *Conclusion*

All that remains to do now is to summarize as briefly as we can some of the main conclusions to which we have come in the course of this chapter:

1. *Modus loquendi apostoli.* Steinbach denies that Augustine and Paul spoke excessively and sees in the distinction between the *modus loquendi apostoli* and the *modus loquendi noster* a means of reconciling some of the more awkward Pauline positions with the theological conclusions of German nominalism. Staupitz agrees that Paul did not take exaggerated positions but is content to accept those positions as they stand and to modify his own theology to conform to the structures of Pauline thought. At the same time he is aware of the limitations of all theological language, both ancient and modern, to encapsulate the mysteries of divine revelation. Still he prefers the biblical modes of thought to the scholastic. Luther agrees with Staupitz and Steinbach that Paul cannot be charged with distorted and exaggerated theological formulations but rejects Steinbach's attempts at reconciliation of Pauline theology with the positions of late scholasticism. Paul's theology is antithetical to the theology of the scholastics and in this clash of warring opinions it is Paul rather than the scholastic doctors who should be followed.

2. *Election.* Steinbach and Staupitz agree that the distinction between conditional and absolute necessity is a useful analytical tool for explaining the nature of predestination and concur in employing the verb *debere* as a middle term between the eternal decision of God to elect and the historical realization of that decision in the justification of the sinner. But whereas Steinbach identifies predestination with prescience, Staupitz rules out foreknowledge of any kind as a qualification to the free and sovereign grace of God. Luther and Staupitz differ over the utility of the distinction between two kinds of necessity but agree that election is absolutely gratuitous. Yet although predestination is the center of Staupitz's thought from which all other graces flow by conditional necessity, election is not so much a center for Luther as it is a safeguard of the freedom of God's promise and the unmerited and gracious character of the human response to it. Luther and Staupitz also concur in pointing to the wounds of Christ as an external ground for certitude of salvation, especially when one is seized with sudden anxiety over one's status with respect to the mystery of election. Neither think highly of *parallelismus practicus* as a basis for certitude.

3. *Justification.* Steinbach, who holds with Staupitz that love is the central principle of justification and who denies that it is possible to be justified by faith alone, regards Abraham as an example of a *viator* who maintained the proper disposition for grace and who merited justification *de congruo* by "doing what was in him." Luther and Staupitz reject the nominalist teaching on preparation for grace (Luther more polemically than Staupitz but not necessarily more thoroughly). Each develops an alternative theory of justification, highly original in many of its features. Both stress in their theories the importance of union with Christ, though they differ over whether the bond of union is faith or love and whether the righteousness which is exchanged is intrinsic or extrinsic. Both agree that the proper preparation for grace is predestination, but do not give it exactly the same function in the structure of their theology as a whole. Staupitz redefines all the key terms in justification in light of what he feels to be the Pauline doctrine of election. Luther, who is convinced that Pauline teaching includes justification by faith alone (illustrated in the career of Abraham, the absolute believer), uses election to secure and safeguard the main lines of that teaching. Luther confesses that the Christian is *iustus et peccator simul* and grounds his present righteousness in the *reputatio Dei*. While Luther's doctrine of sin and grace attempts to take account of the holistic anthropological language of Paul, he continues to agree with Staupitz that virtue is utterly dependent on grace, whatever Biel may teach about *syntheresis*.

Steinbach does not comment on the sacrament of penance in his lectures on Galatians, though if he follows his master, Gabriel Biel, he is a strict contritionist and believes that justifying grace may be given to the genuinely contrite before the administration of the sacrament of the keys. Luther and Staupitz agree with Biel in affirming contrition while rejecting attrition, but their doctrine of contrition is so different that it would be cruelly misleading to stress too much their agreements. For Biel and Steinbach love for God above everything else is the last step in a long process of preparation for grace. For Luther and Staupitz the love of God which creates in the sinner love of justice is the first step in justification. They regard this love entirely as a gift and not in any sense at all as an achievement. Staupitz, who believes that the imperfect contrition of the penitent is made perfect by the sufferings of Christ, is far more conservative than Luther, who holds that faith justifies rather than the sacrament. Luther rejects indulgences while Staupitz only criticizes and restricts them within proper canonical boundaries.

Luther and Staupitz are comrades in a battle, who agree about the main points in their common platform against German nominalism, but who do so for very different—though not antithetical—ideological reasons. When the great controversy with Rome began, that agreement on certain issues and disagreement over others was not strong enough to survive the pressure which was applied to Luther and his disciples. Staupitz was always sympathetic to Luther and wanted to remain a friend, but he lacked sufficient theological motivation to follow Luther into schism. His Augustinianism, while it clashed with the more Pelagian conceptions of grace advocated by Steinbach and Biel, remained comfortably at home within the intellectual structures already provided by medieval Catholicism. Luther's new theology of Word and faith with all its revolutionary consequences for the sacramental life of the Church was too radical for Staupitz, who preferred to read St. Paul with the spectacles provided by the older and more familiar tradition of St. Augustine. That difference led, finally, to a parting of the ways.

V. RELIGIOUS ECSTASY

The relationship of Luther to mysticism is a complex and difficult subject over which much has been written but on which no consensus has been reached.[1] The sheer volume of Luther's writings, on the one hand, and the elusive character of mystical theology, on the other, have conspired to frighten off all but the most intrepid historians. Luther and mysticism is not a subject for the timid and faint-hearted, but by the same token it is not a subject which can endlessly be deferred.

German historians of the late nineteenth and early twentieth centuries tended, on the whole, to denigrate medieval mysticism and to contrast it unfavorably with the purer religion of Martin Luther. Mysticism is, in Karl Holl's phrase, a "subtle search for enjoyment" which builds on the soul's natural kinship with God and which has, depending on the mystical author in question, a more or less seriously defective understanding of sin.[2] Or it is, to follow Erich Seeberg's line of argument, a kind of "methodism," which relies on strict discipline and formalized practices in order to achieve union with God.[3] Emanuel Hirsch singled out the ecstatic God-passion of the medieval mystics as their fatal flaw.[4] The religion of the New Testament is essentially non-ecstatic, as Luther well knew, and the recovery of biblical Christianity necessitates the rejection of all religious ecstasy. Not to be outdone in his distaste for medieval mysticism, Heinrich Bornkamm chided the mystics for their inability to deal with the problem of guilt and their unwarranted desire to obliterate or extinguish the self in God.[5]

Erich Vogelsang moderated these harsh judgments somewhat when he distinguished between three kinds of mysticism—the Dionysian, the Latin,

1. One of the more recent attempts to cover the full range of questions concerning the relationship of Luther to mysticism is the curious study by Bengt R. Hoffman, *Luther and the Mystics* (Minneapolis: Augsburg Publishing House, 1976). Hoffman's book is less an historical study than it is a polemical tract against what Hoffman regards as the excessive rationalism which has dominated Luther research since the age of Lutheran Orthodoxy. What Hoffman prefers is the Luther of Lutheran Pietism, modified somewhat by the insights of Rudolf Otto and Heiko Oberman and set in opposition to the school of Karl Holl. For a fuller assessment of this monograph see my review, "Luther Studies," in *Interpretation* 31 (1977): 305–7.

2. Karl Holl, *Was verstand Luther unter Religion?* (Tübingen, 1917), p. 5.

3. Erich Seeberg, *Grundzüge der Theologie Luthers* (Stuttgart, 1940), p. 33.

4. Emanuel Hirsch, *Das Wesen des reformatorischen Christentums* (Berlin, 1963), pp. 55–67.

5. Heinrich Bornkamm, *Protestantismus und Mystik* (Giessen, 1934), pp. 13–16.

and the German—and indicated that Luther related differently to each of the three different kinds.[6] Luther rejected Dionysian mysticism absolutely after 1516, in spite of the fact that he makes occasional positive references to it. Dionysian mysticism is too speculative for Luther, too impatient with a God who is found in the humiliated and crucified Jesus. Rather the Dionysian mystic wishes to scamper up a graded ladder of ascent to a God who reigns in glory. But the only ladder to God, Luther believes, is the ladder provided by the humanity of Jesus of Nazareth.

While Luther said an unambiguous "no" to Dionysian mysticism, he said both "yes" and "no" to Latin mysticism. Luther approved of its stress on the humanity of Jesus and of its emphasis on experience rather than on mystical theory. He distrusted, however, its use of erotic metaphors and its vision of an ecstatic union with the uncreated Word. He also missed among its exponents any sense of *Anfechtung*, of the desperate inner conflict which the soul sometimes experiences when faith and unbelief hang in the balance.

The German mystics, on the other hand, who, like their Latin counterparts, emphasize the incarnation and the importance of experience, do seem to understand *Anfechtung* and the necessity of despairing of oneself. Luther liked what Tauler and the *Theologia Deutsch* had to say about unconditional resignation to the will of God, about willingness to be damned for the glory of God (*resignatio ad infernum*), and incorporated much of their wisdom into his own discussions of election and certitude of salvation. Luther found in the German mystical writers a genuinely German theological tradition, almost forgotten in squabbles of the warring schools of late scholasticism, but superior to those schools and worthy of recovery.

In an essay read to the Third International Congress for Luther Research in 1966, Heiko Oberman disagreed with Vogelsang's approach to the question of Luther's relationship to the mystics, while acknowledging that Vogelsang's essay in 1936 represented a significant step forward beyond the undifferentiated treatment of medieval mysticism characteristic of earlier Luther scholarship.[7] Still, the typologies which Vogelsang developed do not exactly fit the authors they are intended to describe. Gerson, to take only one obvious example, could as easily fit into the category

6. Erich Vogelsang, "Luther und die Mystik," *Luther-Jahrbuch* 19 (1937): 32–54. See also Vogelsang, "Die unio mystica bei Luther," *ARG* 35 (1938): 63–80.

7. Heiko A. Oberman, "*Simul Gemitus et Raptus*: Luther and Mysticism," in *The Reformation in Medieval Perspective*, ed. Steven E. Ozment (Chicago: Quadrangle Books, 1971), pp. 219–51.

of German mysticism, as Vogelsang describes it, as he does into the category of Latin mysticism, where he seems more naturally to belong.

Oberman proposes, however, not a refinement of Vogelsang's typology but a renunciation of it. One ought to begin with the text of Luther's writings, with the mystical terms and ideas which Luther actually uses, and examine carefully how Luther understands the authorities he cites in support of his own argument. Simply because Luther cites Tauler on *Gelassenheit* (resignation) does not mean that Luther understands this term in exactly the same way as Tauler or that it performs the same function in his theology. The only way to make progress in understanding the relationship of Luther to the mystical tradition is to discover the meaning Luther assigns to those parts of that tradition he actually uses.

When one examines Luther's use of mystical terms, it becomes clear that Luther rejects any mystical formulations which tend to bypass the unique role of Jesus Christ as the Word and Deed of God in history or which exaggerate the possibilities of human cooperation with grace. At the same time Luther so redefines the mystical terms *excessus, raptus,* and *gemitus* that they are made to serve his new theology of faith in the promise of God. Indeed, the absorption is so complete that one could substitute for Luther's formula *iustus et peccator simul* the mystical phrase *simul gemitus et raptus* without any loss of substance. Luther continuously fills the old wineskins of scholastic and mystical theology with a new and heady wine. Excessive reliance on typologies obscures that important fact.

Oberman's suggested approach to mystical theology was adopted by Karl-Heinz zur Mühlen in his book, *Nos Extra Nos: Luthers Theologie zwischen Mystik und Scholastik.*[8] Dr. zur Mühlen, relying particularly on Luther's use of *excessus mentis* in his early exposition of Psalm 115:11, traced the important concept of *extra nos* in Luther's theology back to the idea of mystical ecstasy. That does not mean that Luther is a mystic in the sense that Bernard or Tauler are mystics, but only that he appropriated a central idea from mystical theology, redefined it, and coopted it for his new ideology of Reformation.

I think that Oberman and zur Mühlen are correct in their general approach to the problem of Luther and mysticism.[9] I should like in what

8. Karl-Heinz zur Mühlen, *Nos Extra Nos: Luthers Theologie zwischen Mystik und Scholastik* (Tübingen, 1972), especially pp. 51–66.
9. See also the approach of Darrell R. Reinke, who examines the social meaning of Luther's language in the context of the devotional life of the Erfurt cloister: "Martin Luther: Language and Devotional Consciousness," in *The Spirituality of Western Christendom,* ed. E. R. Elder (Kalamazoo, Mich., 1976), pp. 152–68.

follows to take Luther's early concept of religious ecstasy and show the entirely original way in which Luther redefines this central element of medieval mystical theory and absorbs it into his own rich theology of justification by faith. However, what Luther has in mind will become much clearer if we compare his use of the idea of ecstasy with the teaching of John Staupitz. Staupitz, too, is interested in the relationship between ecstasy and justification, though not exactly in the same way as Luther. If we compare the teaching of these two original thinkers with each other, we shall see, more clearly than if we treated the thought of either in isolation, the new meanings which were being given to the concept of ecstasy in the early sixteenth century in Germany.

1. The Late Medieval Background

John Altenstaig in his massive theological dictionary, published in Hagenau in 1517 and dedicated to John Staupitz, defined religious ecstasy with the help of two fifteenth-century authorities, the French theologian Jean Gerson[10] and the Spanish Augustinian James Perez of Valencia.[11] Gerson's definition is probably more important for Staupitz and Luther, who treasure Gerson's spiritual writings, than is the definition of Perez, though we shall look briefly at both.

Mystical theology for Gerson[12] is an experiential knowledge of God which takes place through the unitive power of love.[13] Speculative theology resides in the intellectual powers whose object is the true, while mystical theology resides in the affective powers whose object is the good.[14] Mystical theology is not rationalistic in the sense that it does not proceed

10. Still the best treatment of the relationship of Gerson and Luther is Steven E. Ozment, *Homo Spiritualis, A Comparative Study of the Anthropology of Johannes Tauler, Jean Gerson and Martin Luther (1509–16) in the Context of their Theological Thought*, SMRT 6 (Leiden, 1969). For Ozment's recent reflections on Luther and mysticism, see his article, "Eckhart and Luther: German Mysticism and Protestantism," *The Thomist* 42 (1978): 259–80.
11. The standard book on Perez is Wilfrid Werbeck, *Jacobus Perez von Valencia, Untersuchungen zu seinem Psalmenkommentar*, Beiträge zur historischen Theologie 28 (Tübingen, 1959).
12. References to Gerson are to the edition, *Ioannis Carlerii de Gerson, De Mystica Theologia*, ed. André Combes (Lugano, 1958), hereafter abbreviated *De myst. Theol.* For a recent treatment of Gerson as a mystic with bibliographical references to Schwab, Ehrle, Dress, Connolly, and Combes, see Heiko A. Oberman, *The Harvest of Medieval Theology* (Cambridge, Mass.: Harvard University Press, 1963), pp. 331–40.
13. Gerson, *De myst. Theol.* I p. 6 cons. 28, 6, p. 72.
14. Gerson, *De myst. Theol.* I p. 6 cons. 29, 2, p. 73.

by a process of deductive reasoning to a theoretical conclusion,[15] and yet it is also not irrational in the sense that it does not dissolve the structures of the mind but elevates the mind's highest powers so that the mind attains the wisdom which transcends theoretical understanding.[16] In short, mystical theology is concerned with union with God. It is concerned with those moments in history when for a brief time the created human spirit becomes one spirit with God through conformity of will.[17] Such a union can only occur in the ecstasy of love.[18]

Ecstasy is a kind of rapture which takes place in the mind or spirit or intelligence.[19] The mind is elevated so that the self's lower powers are suspended in their operation or at least are so weakened that they do not interfere with the activity of the enraptured mind.[20] This ecstatic experience takes place through love and not through the lesser virtues of faith and hope.[21] The presupposition for this ecstatic union is some likeness between God and the purified rational spirit of man.[22] Like is joined to like through the ecstasy of love and by that ecstasy the soul is quieted, satisfied, and stabilized.[23] United to its highest good, what more could the soul want or need?[24] The soul has not lost its being in the Being of God as a drop of water is dissolved in a cask of strong wine, but is intimately united to God by the bond of love.[25]

Whereas Gerson is interested in religious ecstasy as the moment in which the soul is brought to fruition through union with God, James Perez is fascinated by the relationship between ecstasy and revelation.[26] Perez distinguishes three stages of revelation which correspond to the three Latin terms: *excessus*, *extasis*, and *raptus*. *Excessus* is the lowest of the three terms and refers to the inner vision shared by all the prophets when they are cut off from the stimuli of their external senses, are supernaturally illumined in their imaginations, and are made privy to secrets which transcend human reason. *Extasis* represents a still higher stage of

15. Gerson, *De myst. Theol.* I p. 6 cons. 30, 2, p. 76.
16. Gerson, *De myst. Theol.* I p. cons. 30, 3, p. 76.
17. Gerson, *De myst. Theol.* I p. 7 cons. 35, 2, p. 94.
18. Gerson, *De myst. Theol.* I p. 7 cons. 35, 3, pp. 94–95.
19. Gerson, *De myst. Theol.* I p. 7 cons. 36, 2, p. 96.
20. Gerson, *De myst. Theol.* I p. 7 cons. 36, 1, p. 95.
21. Gerson, *De myst. Theol.* I p. 8 cons. 40, 4, p. 104.
22. Gerson, *De myst. Theol.* I p. 8 cons. 41, 17, p. 111.
23. Gerson, *De myst. Theol.* I p. 8 cons. 42, 1, p. 113.
24. Gerson, *De myst. Theol.* I p. 8 cons. 42, 2, p. 113.
25. Gerson, *De myst. Theol.* I p. 8 cons. 41, 1–9, pp. 105–8.
26. The position of Perez is summarized by zur Mühlen, *Nos Extra Nos*, pp. 56–57.

revelation in which the prophet is alienated from his own inner senses and imagination and in his intellect alone sees by means of intelligible species what God wishes him to see and know. This stage of revelation is called ecstasy because in it the prophet is, so to speak, set outside himself, outside the world of inner and outer senses. The third and highest stage of revelation is the state of one who is *raptus*, whose intellect is so elevated that it is granted a vision of the divine essence. This state is so high that it transcends the mere boundaries of prophecy and is accordingly granted to very few persons in this life. In the pages of the New Testament, only Paul reached such an exalted revelatory plateau, while in the old Testament, David reached the stage of extasis and all the prophets without exception share the gift of *excessus mentis*.

In short, as late medieval religious authorities understand it, ecstasy is an elevation of the mind in which the ecstatic person is *supra se* (Gerson)[27] or *extra se* (Perez).[28] It is effected in the mystic and the prophet through the power of divine love and performs two principal functions: (a) it is the act which unites the soul to God and (b) it is the means by which God reveals himself. Without ecstasy there is no revelation and no union with God in this life.

II. *Staupitz on Religious Ecstasy*

Staupitz is not terribly interested in the ecstatic experiences of the prophets. He admits, of course, that Old Testament figures like Job knew Jesus Christ through immediate revelation and one can assume that such revelation must have come through ecstatic inspiration.[29] But one searches the pages of Staupitz's writings in vain for a discussion of the psychology of prophetic ecstasy.

More than that, Staupitz is decidedly skeptical about the claims of contemporary visionaries to have seen in their imagination or through the intelligible species some glimpse of the world beyond. That is not to deny that there are dreams which are authentic revelations. But a true

---

27. See zur Mühlen, *Nos Extra Nos*, p. 60.
28. See zur Mühlen, *Nos Extra Nos*, p. 57.
29. Staupitz, *Hiob* (1497–98) 11.98.32–35. For an introduction to the mystical theology of John Staupitz with a brief survey of the history of scholarship on this question, see my *Misericordia Dei: The Theology of Johannes von Staupitz in its Late Medieval Setting*, SMRT 4 (Leiden: E. J. Brill, 1968), pp. 152–81.

prophet does not receive ecstatic inspirations in order to draw attention to himself or in order to feather his own nest. In 1517 Staupitz ridicules "certain heralds of their own sanctity who boast in a prophetic manner of having various visions. . . . They have seen the omnipotent God the Father as a venerable old man with a beard and innumerable other things which laughter prevents me from reciting."[30]

On the whole, very few visions of this sort, even if they are authentic private revelations, make much, if any, beneficial impact on the Church. If pious people want to see God in this life, they ought not to look for him in dreams and visions and ecstasies, but in the works of charity which do him honor.[31] The non-ecstatic vision of God through good works is enormously more important than the private revelations of a few solitary mystics.[32]

Staupitz wants to talk about ecstasy not as seeing but as tasting.[33] The metaphors which seem to him most appropriate for describing ecstatic experiences are metaphors drawn from the marriage bed[34] and the banqueting table.[35] Ecstasy is a foretaste of the sweetness of final salvation. The pilgrim who experiences such ecstasies of love is strengthened in his faith and motivated to greater conformity to Christ in the conduct of his life. Indeed, Staupitz seems to value ecstasy precisely for its contribution to certitude of salvation[36] and its role in ethical motivation.[37] He does not think much of it as a source of new revelation.

When one compares, however, what Gerson has to say about ecstasy with what Staupitz teaches about it, one discovers striking differences between Staupitz's position and the customary teaching of the late medieval mystics. To begin with, Staupitz separates union with Christ from ecstatic experience. Union with Christ is for Staupitz only another way of talking about justification.

Perhaps I should put that differently: Staupitz distinguishes between two kinds of ecstasy. The first is the experience of the sweetness of the

30. Staupitz, *Libellus* 164. This treatise has recently appeared in a critical edition with footnotes and indices of biblical quotations, citations of theological literature, and a concordance of key Latin and German words. Cf. Johann von Staupitz, *Sämtliche Schriften; Abhandlungen, Predigten, Zeugnisse 2: Lateinische Schriften II*, ed. Lothar Graf zu Dohna, Richard Wetzel et al. (Berlin and New York: Walter de Gruyter, 1979). See my forthcoming review in the *Literaturbericht* of the *ARG* 9 (1980).

31. Staupitz, *Libellus* 169.
32. Staupitz, *Libellus* 166.
33. Staupitz, *Libellus* 110.
34. Staupitz, *Libellus* 120.

35. Staupitz, *Libellus* 150.
36. Staupitz, *Libellus* 62.
37. Staupitz, *Libellus* 53.

love of God which is a special gift of God to some of the elect.[38] But there is another kind of "ecstasy" in which the pilgrim is placed outside himself. This second kind of ecstasy is experienced by every soul which receives justifying grace, even though that soul may not experience any special signs of God's love or taste the sweetness of the coming kingdom of God.[39]

To make clear what Staupitz has in mind, we need to refer again briefly to his theological starting point, the doctrine of election. For Staupitz predestination is a gracious and mysterious act of God which is not motivated by God's prior knowledge of human moral activity and which cannot, no matter how assiduously one attempts to do it, be reduced to simple rational intelligibility. Human salvation begins with and rests at every point on divine election.[40] The gospel is a proclamation, not a divine demand and of the capacities of sinners to meet that demand but rather of the divine initiative which seeks sinners out and which comes to their aid when they despair of their own ability to liberate themselves.

Staupitz's stress on the initiative of God in predestination led him to redefine the doctrine of justification. The entire medieval tradition, and not simply one theological school within it, defined justifying grace or *gratia gratum faciens* as the grace which makes the sinner pleasing to God. This definition seemed to Staupitz to mirror inadequately the nature of God's act. It is not justification but predestination which makes men and women pleasing to God. The function of the grace given in justification is to make God pleasing to the elect.[41]

Justification is simply the fruition in time of a sovereign decree of election made before time. When God chose the elect, he placed Jesus Christ under obligation to give justification to them through his work as mediator.[42] The function of the mediatorial work of Christ is, therefore, not to make men dear to God,[43] but rather to make God dear to men.[44] The elect are the beneficiaries of a covenant which is initiated and fulfilled by God in Jesus Christ.

Justification can also be defined as union with Christ in a spiritual marriage.[45] There is no doubt in Staupitz's mind that the elect will be united to Christ in justification. His conviction in this matter does not rest on any

38. Staupitz, *Libellus* 160–61.
39. Staupitz, *Libellus* 126.
40. Staupitz, *Libellus* 27.
41. Staupitz, *Libellus* 131.

42. Staupitz, *Libellus* 22, 26, 27, 33.
43. Staupitz, *Libellus* 36, 40, 86, 131, 152.
44. Staupitz, *Lieb Gottes*, Kn. 105.
45. Staupitz, *Libellus* 76–77.

illusions about the merit of the elect or the stability of their faith,[46] but is based rather on his conviction that God will be faithful to his decree of election.[47] The calling of the elect, their justification, their restoration to conformity to Christ, and their final glorification are all covenanted mercies of God given unconditionally to the elect.[48] But ecstasy, in the sense of a foretaste of the sweetness of divine love, is not a covenanted mercy of God owed to all the elect. All the elect are sooner or later united to Christ in justification, but only some of the elect are granted ecstatic foretastes of the heavenly banquet at the end of time. God is a debtor to the elect of union with Christ, but a giver of spiritual ecstasy. Union is owed; ecstasy is not.[49]

However, if union with Christ is synonymous with justification, then the presupposition for such union is not likeness to God but unlikeness. The candidate for union is not someone who has undergone a long process of spiritual discipline or who comes into the presence of God purged, illumined, trembling with holy modesty. The candidate for union is a sinner. Indeed, it is his sin which qualifies him for union with Christ. Only he must become a "real sinner," someone who despairs of himself and his own abilities to justify himself and who throws himself utterly on the mercy of God.[50]

It is precisely at this point that Staupitz introduces the theme of ecstasy in the sense of "seizing someone," of "placing someone entirely outside himself." This ecstatic removal of the self from itself, this alienation of the self from its own powers, occurs for Staupitz in two stages. First of all, the demand of God in its radical intensity—what Staupitz calls the law of Christ according to the letter—places the sinner outside himself in the sense of total self-despair.[51] The soul is torn from its old reliance on itself by the law of God. But the law alienates the self from itself in order that grace may unite the self to Christ.[52] The ecstatic self is the self married to Christ through love. This ecstasy is synonymous with the first moment of justification and is not at all to be confused with the spiritual heights of love which God grants to a few of the elect.

Such ecstasy is more valued by Staupitz than either private visions or experiences of joy in God's love, because it always leads to a change in the pattern of one's behavior. By virtue of this ecstasy every Christian is one

46. Staupitz, Libellus 26.
47. Staupitz, Libellus 62.
48. Staupitz, Libellus 19.
49. Staupitz, Libellus 161.
50. Staupitz, Nachfolgung, Kn. 86.
51. Staupitz, Libellus 126.
52. Staupitz, Libellus 129–31.

spirit, one will with Christ. This ecstasy is essential to Christian existence as experiences of rapture in the traditional sense are not. No one is a Christian who has not been alienated from himself and inserted into Christ. So while Staupitz views ecstasy as private revelation with suspicion, makes ecstasy as a foretaste of the sweetness of divine love an important but not essential gift outside the covenanted mercies of God, he nevertheless regards ecstasy in this third sense as basic to his understanding of the justification of the sinner.

III. *Young Luther on Religious Ecstasy*

Luther's teaching on religious ecstasy can only be understood correctly if it is placed in its proper context. It will not do to plunge into a consideration of ecstasy without reviewing some of the more important presuppositions which underlie Luther's earliest theological work, especially his massive commentary on the Psalms.

Luther's lectures on the Psalms describe and celebrate the threefold work of God in Christ, in the Church, and in the individual Christian.[53] What is central for Luther, the work of God for the salvation of the world in Jesus Christ, is underscored by Luther's stress on the literal-prophetic meaning of the Psalms.[54] Luther is not interested in the literal-historical meaning of the Psalms—the mere story told by the words—or in compiling information about the cultic and liturgical practices of ancient Israel. He is interested in the relation of each psalm to the work of God in Christ and in the significance of that work for the Christian who stands in the present, rather far removed from the original setting in which such a psalm was composed. In short, Luther wants to stress both the literal-prophetic sense of Scripture and its tropological significance.[55]

This saving work of God in Christ is considered by Luther as a drama in time with three critical moments: the advent of Christ in the flesh,[56] and his subsequent advents in grace[57] and in glory.[58] All three advents are closely tied together. Christ destroyed the glory of the world through the humility of his first advent in order to dispense his grace to sinners through his second advent, the event of faith. The advent of Christ in

53. WA 3.369.2–10; 4.189.4ff.; 3.541.38–542.2.   55. WA 3.351.33–37; 3.532.23–26.
54. WA 4.305.6–12; 55¹.8.8–11.   56. WA 3.523.21–31.
57. WA 3.625.29–34; 4.19.31–36; 4.94.32–33.
58. WA 3.625.29–34.

glory refers to the future completion of the work of God begun in the humility of the incarnation and continued in the act of faith.

According to Isaiah 28, the God who acts in Christ, in the Church, and in the faithful soul does both a strange (*opus alienum*) and a proper work (*opus proprium*).[59] The strange work of God is his wrath; the proper work, his mercy. The two activities are not coordinate but stand in a dialectical relationship to each other. Just as the first advent of Christ was for the sake of his second, so, too, the strange work of God takes place for the sake of his proper work. While final impenitence and damnation are terrifying possibilities for the sinner (Luther is no Origen and does not envision a cosmological reconciliation of wrath and mercy), nevertheless wrath is meant to be God's penultimate rather than his final word.

In a similar fashion Luther distinguishes between the wrath of severity (*ira severitatis*) and the wrath of mercy (*ira misericordiae*).[60] While the impenitent taste the severe wrath of God, the elect suffer from the wrath whose ultimate intention is merciful. God destroys the old reality which he has remorselessly consigned to dissolution in order to build something new and better in its place. The Word of God, therefore, first executes God's alien work and, only when that is accomplished, sets in motion his proper work.[61]

One cannot contemplate the work of God celebrated in the Psalms without stumbling across the fact that such divine activity is both hidden and revealed. Like Dionysius, Luther is struck by the hiddenness of God and the superiority of negative theology over positive. But there the similarities end and the differences begin to multiply. The work of God is hidden, not because God is trancendent and dwells in thick darkness (though there is a sense in which Luther is willing to say even that), but because faith deals with "things which do not appear" (*res non apparentes*).

Luther's reflections over Hebrews 11:1 with its definition of faith as an evidence of "things unseen" should not be read through Neo-platonic spectacles, though there may be a trace of Platonism in what Luther says. The object of faith is invisible for two reasons, neither of which has very much to do with Plato. The object of faith is invisible either because it is future (no one, after all, can see next Wednesday) or because it is hidden from empirical observation in the present under the form of a contrary

59. *WA* 3.245.41ff.; 4.87.22–25.
60. *WA* 55¹.40.16; 3.153.30–32; 3.439.29–31.
61. *WA* 3.330.26–28.

appearance.[62] As Paul confesses in his first letter to Corinth (1:18–31)—a passage of extreme importance for the young Luther—God delights to reveal his strength in weakness, his wisdom in what the world regards as utter folly.

In other words, it is not apparent to sight that Jesus is anything more than an untutored carpenter executed by the Romans on trumped-up charges; or that the Church is anything more than a collection of precisely those people whom one tries desperately the other six days of the week not to meet; or that the believer is anything more than a frightened, fallible, and sinful mortal, not much different from his neighbors who profess no religious belief. Yet the Bible against reason and common sense claims that the martyred carpenter is the Savior of the world, that the Church is his mystical body, and that the individual believer is such an object of divine mercy and love that the angels (if they could indulge in envy) would be jealous of him. The presence of God in Christ, in the Church, and in the individual soul is discerned, not by sight, but by hearing the word of promise which contradicts the evidence which the eye can see and by trusting it.[63]

It is against the background of these presuppositions that Luther talks about religious ecstasy. The question we need to answer now is whether we find in Luther the three forms of religious ecstasy we found in Staupitz—ecstasy as prophetic inspiration, as a foretaste of final salvation, and as the normal response of the sinner to justifying grace—and, if so, whether Luther understands them in the same way as Staupitz. It is a difficult question and we can only sketch in a very brief answer to it. The gist of the answer will be that Luther is very interested in ecstasy as a sudden illumination of the mind and as the normal state of the justified sinner, but that he is not terribly interested in ecstasy as a nuptial feast to which only a few contemplatives are invited.

The principal locus for Luther's earliest reflections on religious ecstasy is his commentary on Psalm 115 [116], especially verses 11 and 15, in his *Dictata super Psalterium.* The occasion for Luther's extended comments is provided by the opening words of verse 11: *Ego dixi in excessu meo: omnis homo mendax.* Luther interprets these words as a reference to *excessus mentis* or *exstasis:* "I said in my ecstasy: every man is a liar."

62. WA 55[1].20.13–15; 55[2].106.16–19; 3.127.19–24; 3.311.35–36; 4.81.25–27; 4.337.10–12.
63. WA 3.548.2–5; 4.95.1–4; 4.356.9–13; 3.651.19–22; 4.83.3–9.

In his gloss on the text Luther suggests four possible meanings of ecstasy in this verse.[64] The psalmist may be referring to the *sensus fidei*, the spiritual meaning of the prophecy, which exceeds the merely literal sense of the words of the prophet (to which all unbelievers, who lack spiritual discernment, invariably cling). Or it may refer to ecstasy in the proper sense, a *raptus mentis*, which brings one's mind to the clear knowledge of faith. It can also have reference to the fearful and disturbed state of mind of a believer who suffers persecution or to the mystical experiences of Christ and the martyrs. As Luther makes clear in his three comments on Psalm 115:11 in his scholion, it is ecstasy in the second and third senses, as *raptus mentis in claram cognitionem fidei* and as *alienatio seu pavor mentis in persecutione*, which interests him most. It is also clear that he is less interested in the ecstasy of the prophet than he is in the sudden perception of the believer through faith of his situation in relation to God (*coram Deo*) with its consequent implications for his relationship to others (*coram hominibus*); namely, *omnis homo mendax*.

Religious ecstasy is not merely affective for Luther; it is cognitive.[65] But the cognition is granted to faith and is mediated by the Word of God.[66] The believer suddenly perceives that what God says is true, though reason and sense may contradict it, and trusts that Word rather than his own resources or the aid of other people who stand around him. Persecution is the situation par excellence in which one learns that human help is vain and that one should trust the Word of God alone. Faith elevates and exalts the self *coram Deo*. What earlier mystics and teachers, including Staupitz, had attributed to divine love is now attributed by Luther to faith. *Si enim credidit, coram deo exaltatus est: fides enim elevat.*[67] The ecstasy of faith elevates one beyond oneself so that one can see the future goods promised to faith, the so-called "things that do not appear."[68]

Luther views the believer as simultaneously (*simul*) ecstatic and humiliated, exalted and in consternation.[69] The self knows itself in the ecstasy of faith as a sinner and so is radically humbled before God. The more one trusts the promises of God, the less one is inclined to trust oneself. One knows by faith that the judgment, *omnis homo mendax*, applies to the self as well as to others. The ecstasy of faith excludes in principle all schemes of self-justification through good works.

64. *WA* 4.265.30–36.   65. *WA* 4.265.32ff.
66. A point emphasized by zur Mühlen, *Nos Extra Nos*, p. 65.
67. *WA* 4.271.2.   69. *WA* 4.273.19–21.
68. *WA* 4.275.14.

The presupposition for religious ecstasy is not likeness to God, not syntheresis, not a process of ascetic discipline and self-denial, but faith alone.[70] Ecstasy for Luther as for Staupitz before him is inseparable from the question of the justification of the sinner. God's promises are offered, not to aristocrats of the Spirit, but to real sinners. "Real sinners" are people who know by faith that they are sinners, who accuse themselves and who justify God in his condemnation of them.[71] But everyone who is humiliated by faith in the Word of God is simultaneously exalted and sees by faith "the things which do not appear." Humility and ecstasy coincide. *Excessus mentis* is a description of every soul who is justified by faith.

Luther agrees with Staupitz that it is in the first moment of justification that the believer is joined to Christ in a spiritual marriage, though he does not really develop this theme in the *Dictata* as fully as in his later writings.[72] The believer is married to Christ in faith and that bond of union becomes the basis of an exchange of sin and righteousness between Christ and the Christian.

I said earlier that religious ecstasy for Luther was cognitive and not merely affective. But we shall misunderstand Luther seriously if we interpret the *excessus mentis* which leads to the clear knowledge of faith as something which is exclusively cognitive. It is also, as the scholion to Psalm 64:2 asserts, dumb amazement in the presence of a mystery which can be experienced but never reduced to dogmatic and rational propositions.[73] Faith elevates the mind to rapture and ecstasy, or, as Luther insists, to supreme repose and silence as well. Faith penetrates the cloud beyond thinking and speaking where God dwells.

By praising negative theology, however, Luther does not mean to commend speculative theology which attempts to bypass the incarnation and the revelation of God in history. The centrality of the incarnation for Luther has been evident ever since his marginal notes on Augustine and Peter Lombard composed in 1509–10.[74] The cloud which ecstatic faith must penetrate is the revelation of God hidden in the humanity of Jesus of Nazareth. In his lectures on Hebrews in 1517 Luther makes that conviction even more explicit when he writes: "For the humanity [of Christ] is the sacred ladder by which we ascend to the knowledge of God."[75] He

---

70. *WA* 4.271.2.
71. *WA* 3.288.6–32; 3.291.26–28; 55^2.24.6–12; 55^2.33.1–4.
72. *WA* 3.211.23–35; 3.142.26–30; 55^2.105.6–9.
73. *WA* 3.372.7ff.   75. *BoA* 5.345.4–5.
74. *WA* 9.17.12; 9.23.30; 9.39.32.

repeats this theme in 1520 in a sermon on the assumption of Mary: "Every ascent to the knowledge of God is dangerous beyond the ascent which takes place through the humanity of Christ, because this humanity is Jacob's ladder, by which one should ascend."[76]

Luther joins ecstasy and justification by faith, exaltation and humiliation, hiddenness and revelation, incarnation and ascent, *excessus mentis* and *pavor mentis*, cognition and silent astonishment in a dizzyingly original combination. Like Staupitz and unlike Gerson, Luther is concerned to develop an understanding of the central role of religious ecstasy in the justification of the sinner. Like Perez and unlike Staupitz, Luther is fascinated with the illumination of the mind which takes place in ecstasy. Unlike Staupitz, Gerson, and Perez, Luther associates religious ecstasy with faith rather than with love.

Of all the theorists of religious ecstasy whom we have mentioned Luther is most like Staupitz. His emphasis on the ecstatic state of the justified sinner, on union with Christ as the foundation rather than the fruition of the Christian life, on "real sin" rather than on likeness to God as the presupposition for ecstatic union, and on the coincidence of exaltation and humiliation in the experience of justification mark him as an ally, if not disciple, of Staupitz in his spiritual teaching. But Luther attributes ecstasy to faith and Staupitz to love. Staupitz belongs, finally, to the older Augustinian tradition which emphasizes the priority of love over faith in the process of justification. Luther, however, has begun to redefine all the traditional concepts—including the language of mystical theology—in the light of his new understanding of the meaning of faith. How revolutionary that difference was at the time of the composition of the *Dictata super Psalterium* did not become immediately apparent, even to Luther himself. What Luther had done, however, even in his early pre-Reformation writings, was to lay the basis for an emerging Protestant spirituality. The truly spiritual person, as Luther points out in his marginal notes on John Tauler (1516), is the person who relies on faith.[77] That is a theological shift of great importance in the history of Western Christianity.

---

76. *BoA* 5.431.14–16. For the philosophical background of the language of ascent and descent and for an extensive bibliography of this and related problems, see the forthcoming important article by Edward P. Mahoney, "Metaphysical Foundations of the Hierarchy of Being according to Some Late Medieval and Renaissance Philosophers," in *Ancient and Medieval Philosophies of Existence*, ed. Parviz Morewedge (New York: Fordham University Press, 1981).

77. *WA* 9.103.37ff.

VI. CONCLUSION

It may seem at first glance as if the results of this study have been largely negative. Most of the suggestions which have been made by historians about the relationship of Luther to Staupitz—that Staupitz is the mediator of a late medieval Augustinian school tradition to Luther (Oberman), or that Luther was a disciple of Staupitz in his earliest approach to the interpretation of the Bible (Bauer) or in his first articulation of his doctrine of justification (Bizer)—seem to me not to be justified by the documentary evidence. Luther's understanding of Word and faith, his reluctance to make election the center of his thought, and his tendency to subject traditional modes of thought to a radical critique set him apart from Staupitz, who, for all his theological originality, is content to follow a more traditional and well-marked path established by generations of conservative Augustinian theologians.

Nor is Wolf's judgment that Staupitz was an important stimulus for Luther during the crucial years in which he was forging the central themes of his new theology an adequate description of their relationship. It is, of course, a true judgment. There are a number of important ideas which appear in Luther's thought because they were first taught by Staupitz. When Luther pointed timid souls towards the wounds of Christ for consolation when they were terrified by anxieties concerning election, when he insisted that real sin is the sole precondition for the reception of grace, when he taught that penance begins with the love of God, when he described the normal response of the justified sinner to the presence of grace as "ecstatic," he was repeating themes which he himself had learned in conversation with Staupitz, however much Luther may have modified these themes to fit the larger structure of his thought. In that sense at least, Luther was always a Staupitzian in his theology.

This study set out to measure the degree of influence John Staupitz exercised on the theological formation of the young Martin Luther. What it succeeded in demonstrating was the astonishing degree of independence from his teachers Luther exhibited from the very beginning. Luther is always more than the sum of the parts of his theological heritage. His first lectures on the Psalms comprise a highly original work, unified in theme if not in development, which neither John Staupitz nor John of Paltz— nor even Gregory of Rimini—could have written. Luther learned from

Staupitz, Trutfetter, Biel, and Paltz as Beethoven learned from Mozart, Haydn, and Bach. But the first work of each carries an original and unforgettable stamp.

Not only is the young Luther a theological genius whose work cannot be explained as the inevitable product of a series of interlocking causes and subtle influences—even if those causes and influences do exist and can be traced—but there is as well a consistency about his work, a steady development of his major and subdominant themes, which links his work before the Reformation to his work as one of the primary intellectual leaders of early Protestantism. Old Luther tried to argue that there was an abrupt shift, a diastasis between his pre-Reformation writings and his later work.[1] There is, however, no evidence of such a radical shift, though plenty of evidence of growth and development. Luther takes up new ideas and drops old ones. He does that until the day of his death. But these shifts take place within a larger framework which remains remarkably constant over the course of his whole life.

I do not contest the right of old Luther to practice revisionist historiography on his early life and to heighten and exaggerate the discontinuities between his earlier and his later thought. It was, after all, his life and he was free to remember and evaluate it as he chose. But just as historians dare not accept at face value Luther's recollections and evaluations of his contemporaries, whether of Erasmus, Bucer, Carlstadt, Staupitz, Melanchthon, Cajetan, Eck, or Zwingli, shrewd and witty as those evaluations undoubtedly are, so, too, historians ought not ingenuously to accept Luther's own flawed and revised memories of his early life without testing those memories against the surviving documentary evidence. The evidence we have examined argues against diastasis and for continuity. Just because Luther in an allusion to Ovid referred to his early theology as "a crude and inchoate muddle"[2] is no reason that we should feel obliged to agree with him, especially when our own reading of his early works demonstrates the marvelous complexity of his mind and the thoroughly self-consistent character of his central arguments.

But though Luther was independent, he was still influenced by John Staupitz. Staupitz's primary importance for Luther was, as Luther himself always insisted, pastoral in nature. Staupitz gave Luther the courage and

1. For an interesting discussion of this question and of the use to which historians have put Luther's reflections, see Ian D. K. Siggins, *Martin Luther's Doctrine of Christ* (New Haven, Conn.: Yale University Press, 1970), pp. 1–11.
2. *WA* 54.179.2–12.

opportunity to face what he feared. Luther was terrified by certain words. In 1518 he said the word was "penance" and in 1545 "righteousness." He was terrified by them because he feared that lurking behind them he might find a hidden God, more frightening than anything he could have imagined. Like a man who worries that he may have a serious illness but refuses to see a physician, Luther averted his eyes from what he feared, content rather to bear those ills he had than, by looking too closely at his fears, to discover that they were only harmless shadows of a nameless Dread.

Staupitz perceived that Luther's psychological anxieties were caused by his bad theology. It was not unresolved problems with his father[3]—however serious those problems might be—but unresolved problems with his image of God which drove Luther to despair. Staupitz frontally attacked that bad theology and so helped Luther to resolve his anxieties by administering a therapeutic combination of traditional pastoral advice with sound Augustinian theology. The traditional advice helped Luther to perceive the gracious intention of the Church's discipline and the Augustinian theology corrected Luther's nominalist understanding of grace and justification. The two together did not resolve all of Luther's problems but they gave him sufficient courage to master his fears and to think through for himself what the Bible meant by righteousness, repentance, grace, and faith.

Staupitz, of course, took no chances with his faint-hearted younger brother. He lashed him to the mast by exacting from him as a matter of obedience the promise to earn his doctorate in theology and to assume the chair of biblical studies at Wittenberg. Staupitz exacted that promise because he had a relaxed and unlimited confidence in the mercy of God, on the one hand, and a real, if qualified, confidence in the ability of his talented younger brother to seize that mercy, on the other.

I am inclined, therefore, to take with very great seriousness Luther's confession that he would have continued to mope in a hell of unresolved anxiety without the pastoral advice of Staupitz and that Staupitz was—in this sense at least—the originator of Protestant doctrine. Staupitz was no Protestant and the split between Luther and Staupitz after 1518 does

3. For a collection of important essays dealing with Erik Erikson's thesis concerning the relationship of Luther with his father, see Roger A. Johnson, ed., *Psychohistory and Religion: The Case of Young Man Luther* (Philadelphia: Fortress Press, 1977). For a fresh perspective on Luther's relationship to his parents, see the fascinating essay by Ian D. K. Siggins, "Luther's Mother Margarethe," *HTR* 71 (1978): 125–50.

not come as a complete surprise. But Staupitz put Luther on the road to Reformation by his effective work as a pastor. Staupitz corrected Luther's theology and, even more importantly, gave Luther the encouragement he needed to wrestle with the great issues of the Christian faith. Apart from Staupitz there might very well have occurred a Protestant Reformation. The time was certainly ripe for some kind of reform in the Church, Erasmian or Hussite or Conciliar. But the Reformation which occurred would not have had Martin Luther as one of its principal leaders. It would have had a different character and a different outcome. To concede that, however, is to admit that Staupitz was, in a way that Goch or Wesel or Gansfort or Wyclif could never be, an essential forerunner of the Reformation.

INDEX